SUBURBAN GRINDHOUSE

ISSUE TWO

-Searching for Utopia with FANDO Y LIS and GLEN AND RANDA

-SUBURBAN GRINDHOUSE MEMORIES no 81: "It's Clobberin' Time!"

-MIDNIGHT MOVIES: America's Most Bizarre Subculture Lives On

-WITHOUT A STITCH: Scandalous Drive-In Classic

-Satan in the 70s: Occult Cinema Explosion

-Films / Blu-rays / Streaming / Theatrical Screenings

-Books / Zines / Novels

1974-2024: Films Celebrating their 50th Anniversaries

Still, in my humble opinion, the *scariest* film of all time, THE TEXAS CHAINSAW MASSACRE headed the 50th anniversaries in 2024, celebrated around the globe, most notably at the Museum of Modern Art in NYC where it screened for a week in August in a restored 4K version (see my review in the main film section).

Also, THE ANTICHRIST, THE BLOODY EXORCISM OF COFFIN JOE, DEATHDREAM, DERANGED, FRIGHTMARE, THE HOUSE OF SEVEN CORPSES, HOUSE OF WHIPCORD, IMPULSE, IT'S ALIVE!, LET SLEEPING CORPSES LIE, LISA AND THE DEVIL, SUGAR HILL, VAMPYRES, COCKFIGHTER, DEATH WISH, THE LORDS OF FLATBUSH, THE GODFATHER PART 2, PHANTOM OF THE PARADISE, THE NIGHT PORTER, CAGED HEAT, DIRY MARY AND CRAZY LARRY, STREET LAW, SHOOT FIRST-DIE LATER, ALMOST HUMAN, FOXY BROWN, GODZILLA VS. MECHAGODZILLA, BLAZING SADDLES, YOUNG FRANKENSTEIN, THE GROOVE TUBE, BLACK BELT JONES, MASSACRE MAFIA STYLE, EMERGENCY SQUAD … and of course many more, but these are in the general interest of SUBURBAN GRINDHOUSE's main readership. Give 'em a watch…

Unless otherwise noted, all text by Nick Cato, ©2024 RetroZines Ltd.
This issue is dedicated to Dennis Daniel and 42nd Street Pete

SEARCHING FOR UTOPIA WITH
FANDO Y LIS AND GLEN AND RANDA

In Alejandro Jodorowsky's lesser-seen debut feature, FANDO Y LIS (1968), a couple travel across a post-nuclear wasteland in search of a mystical city rumored to hold the key to their ailments. Lis is paralyzed, and her lover Fando seems to be impotent, or at least incapable of performing his manly duties. Fando carries Liz on his back, until finding a cart to push her on. A surreal journey film, it was a template for the director's two films to come as both EL TOPO (1970) and THE HOLY MOUNTAIN (1973) are centered around quests. But the search for a utopian environment is arguably more surreal here, as our protagonists meet an endless array of people, each one stranger than the last.

GLEN AND RANDA (1971) deals with the teenaged title characters, living like Adam and Eve in an isolated wooded area twenty-plus years after a nuclear holocaust. They've been surviving with a small group and have never seen anything outside their community, nor do they have any knowledge of the earth before it was nuked. After being visited by an older man known only as The Magician, Glen receives a Wonder Woman comic book as a gift and is convinced there's a real city called Metropolis, where people fly and everyone dresses in white. He persuades Randa to join him in searching for it, and The Magician gives him a map to get there.

Unlike Fando Y Lis, Glen and Randa only encounter one other person on their journey, who also happens to be an older man named Sidney. Discovering Randa is pregnant, he brings them to his seaside residence, which is a rundown trailer home. One of the bleakest of the era's end-time films, GLEN AND RANDA pictures a future where the new generation are uneducated, only a step away from turning back to a neanderthal-like mindset. The only thing keeping Glen going is the hope of finding Metropolis, an obsession he can't seem to fully implant in Randa, or his new friend, the elderly Sidney.

The road to utopia in FANDO Y LIS is paved with predators: the couple is continually confronted by self-imposed elitists, religious zealots, drag queens, and old ladies who give the modern "hag horror" subgenre a run for its money. While Fando deals with many of the physical assaults, Lis' psychological anguish is never-ending. Not only can she not make her away around in the flesh without Fando's help, she also mentally can't bring herself to leave him, even with his continual abuse (this film would most likely be *cancelled* today after one public screening). And while our couple never find the legendary city of Tar, the director deals with resurrection in a way only he could pull off ... at least at the time this film was created.

On their non-surreal journey, GLEN AND RANDA's excursion is interrupted not by bizarre characters, but normal circumstances, mainly Randa's pregnancy. When she dies during childbirth, Sidney becomes Glen's new traveling companion. All throughout Randa's pregnancy, Glen is most concerned about making it to Metropolis. The Magician calls him out on his obsession before he leaves the safety of his home camp. Randa hides her annoyance of his continually talking about it by trying to get Glen to care about their provisions and lodgings. But Glen is singularly focused, a picture of the hippie peace and love movement leaving its skin behind for the coming self-obsessed yuppie/Generation X.

Utopia is never found in either film. Glen's preoccupation with it leads to Randa's demise, and the director chose to leave the ending up to the viewer as to what they believe about him: has Sidney's boat sunk on their trek to Metropolis? Has Sidney done Glen a favor, knowing the world had been destroyed, and threw him overboard, keeping the baby to be raised by a sane person? Or did the elements take the three travelers into oblivion? The final shots of the film are as beautiful as they are haunting, but whatever fate the viewer is comfortable with, its apparent paradise was not to be found.

While Glen and Randa at least had a roadmap (although it's apparent neither knew how to read it), Fando Y Lis travel to Tar without any knowledge of how to get there. It's funny how, during their journey, Fando asks Lis if they're on the right path, as if someone unable to walk would know any more than he does. Again, this is Jodorowsky, and every line of dialogue can be taken as metaphor. But our couple seem to be going in circles, albeit encountering new groups of people at every turn. The director's lifelong fascination with Catholicism and the Messiah point to Fando Y Lis finding utopia *in resurrection*. As for an earthly place, it's not to be found here, and the audience is not given the alternative satisfaction Jodorowsky would offer five years later in THE HOLY MOUNTAIN's controversial finale.

Our four travelers, within these two films, held different degrees of hope of finding a better place. Some were obsessed. Some were worried about leaving the small comforts of their lonely existences. Some were happy or at least at peace with their place in the world. But none found what they were looking for or what was promised to them.

Perhaps these celluloid journeys *themselves*, in their own bizarre way, are the film aficionado's means of finding those mystical places...

(Fando pushes his lover Lis through a post-nuclear wasteland on a musical cart)

SUBURBAN GRINDHOUSE MEMORIES no 81:
"It's Clobberin' Time!"

After being assaulted by prime time and late-night TV commercials, my interest was piqued for THE HOUSE WHERE DEATH LIVES, a film where, going just by its ad campaign, was hard to tell if it was a slasher or supernatural offering. It turns out neither, although since its release some have labeled it a pseudo-slasher. But by the time you finish reading this column you just may agree with me and consider it a sleep-inducing turkey. And in 1984, there were A LOT of sleep-inducing turkeys out there.

Once again, the Amboy Twin (now the site of a Mexican restaurant) admitted my friends and I to a Saturday afternoon screening with just about half the theater filled up. Of course, I was the only geek in attendance who recognized Patricia Pearcy (the actress who starred in the far superior 1976 creep-fest SQUIRM) as soon as she walked onscreen, yet any hope I had for this flick ended just minutes later.

Meredith (Pearcy) is an in-home nurse who arrives at the mansion of an ill millionaire named Ivar Langrock (played by Joseph Cotten, who also starred in a superior horror film, 1980's THE HEARSE, among dozens of others). She's there to take care of him in his last days, and is joined by Ivan's creepy, flaky, nerdy grandson Gabriel (who played one of the teens in JAWS 2 (1978)), and Ivar's lawyer, Jeffrey (David Hayward, who had roles in Tobe Hooper's EATEN ALIVE (1976) and VAN NUYS BLVD. (1979) among others). For most of the film, we hear Meredith narrating the story through her thoughts, but unlike 1972's SILENT NIGHT, BLOODY NIGHT, which employed this technique in a minor way and to far better effect, here it comes off as silly and had most of the crowd giggling and yelling for her to "Shit or get off the pot" (yep, this was actually blurted out by someone sitting close to the screen). After a while I wondered if she'd ever start talking with her mouth, and eventually she did (but we get more thinking narration before long). Ughh.

To break up the tediousness, visitors and butlers/maids are being killed off, and everyone is a suspect. In the finale, when the killer is revealed, said killer beats the living crap out of someone with a chair leg, which was the only thing in the film that earned slight applause from the audience who I assume were a bored as I was (if not for the Goldberg's Dark Chocolate Chews and their wonderful sugar level, I'm sure even at 15 years of age I would've dozed off). And speaking of beating people to death, I'd like to take a chair leg to the cranium of whoever gave this turd an R rating. The clubbings are more graphic in your average Bugs Bunny cartoon, there's barely any blood spilled, and the "sex scene" is quick and shot quite dark, hence nothing is shown. Even a scene where Gabriel walks into the bathroom as Meredith bathes shows nothing, making THE HOUSE WHERE DEATH LIVES an easy PG. But, in 1984, as it is today, R rated films sold more tickets, so…

The crowd at the Amboy Twin, along with my buds and myself, left the theater completely unsatisfied. This heavily advertised sleep-fest was more of a murder mystery TV movie of the week than an R rated slasher or haunted house film, and like many films released in the early-mid 80s featured a newspaper ad / theater poster that was way better than the film itself.

I recently revisited the film on YouTube after writing this column, and I have to say it was even more boring than I remembered. There's a side plot about Meredith being sexually abused by her father I didn't recall (most likely because it adds little to the plot), and regardless of her fine turn in SQUIRM, here Patricia Pearcy's acting was, shall we say, less than stellar. Not bad, but for a leading lady in a widely released film, less than stellar. And I had forgotten all about one decent scene toward the ending, where Ivar pulls a predictable yet fun surprise on Meredith, but in the end, I think everyone at the Amboy Twin knew who the killer was from early on. The real victims at this screening were us, the suburban audience, who were lured into the theater thanks to a slick TV commercial and a newspaper ad campaign that was 99.9% FALSE.

The film was (first) released theatrically in 1981 and on VHS as DELUSION, I don't think it ever came to DVD, and I'm sure it's only a matter of time until it comes out as a deluxe blu-ray (**UPDATE**: It's now in 4K thanks to the loonies sat Vinegar Syndrome) to steal the moolah of unsuspecting newbies. If it does, they should at least re-title it THE HOUSE WHERE SLEEP LIVES, because that's what viewers will surely be doing shortly after the opening credits. I'll assume this was specifically titled for its 1984 theatrical re-release to cash in on the (then) slasher craze?

Either way, for Nytol completists only.

(Note: The first 79 editions of this column are collected in the book SUBURBAN GRINDHOUSE: FROM STATEN ISLAND TO TIMES SQUARE AND ALL THE SLEAZE BETWEEN by Nick Cato, available at Headpress.com, Amazon, and all well-hung booksellers)

MIDNIGHT MOVIES:
AMERICA'S MOST BIZARRE SUBCULTURE LIVES ON

(Ad from the Village Voice circa 1982: when the 8th Street Playhouse ran midnight movies 7 nights a week)

The phenomenon known as the *Midnight Movie* stretches as far back as the 1930s, although at that time it existed for different reasons than it would years later. A simple Internet search can tell you some of what you need to know about pre-1970 midnight movie screenings, and books such as Stuart Samuels' MIDNIGHT MOVIES (1983 Collier Books) provides what I consider a definitive look at the Golden Era of the movement (which ran from approximately 1970-1982). In J. Hoberman and Jonathan Rosenbaum's MIDNIGHT MOVIES (1991 Da Capo Press), the authors go on to look at over 100 films that have either played or been connected to midnight screenings, and both authors were pivotal in certain films covered in their book surviving as midnight features. It is commonly noted that New York's Elgin Theater, on December 18th, 1970, began the midnight movie craze as it is known today with their screening of *El Topo*, which not only grew a devout midnight following, but played there seven days a week for seven months. In my own experience as a fan of midnight movies, here in New York City, late night screenings managed to survive, somewhat, after the end of the Golden Era. They continued in some capacity throughout the 1980s and into the 1990s, and in the mid-2000s thanks mainly to NYC's Two Boots Pioneer theater and their sold-out screenings of *Donnie Darko* (more on that later). But, midnight screenings returned with a vengeance around 2010 thanks in large part to a few upstart theaters run by ardent film fans.

This is mainly my personal account of midnight movies in and around New York City. The phenomenon has existed in many American cities, as well as theaters around the world. Often, certain theaters featured "midnight classics" such as *The Rocky Horror Picture Show, Pink Flamingos, El Topo, Eraserhead*, and more recently, films such as *The Room* and *Pulp Fiction*. Hence, while the features may change, it seems to be universally agreed upon which films appeal to midnight audiences.

Also of note are programs such as "Midnight Madness", which is part of the TIFF (Toronto International Film Festival), and late-night film programs held at colleges around the country.

My personal journey into this world which author Stuart Samuels dubbed "America's Most Bizarre Subculture" began when I was in the fifth grade, sometime in 1978 or 1979. A girl in my class had come to school wearing a black t-shirt with big red lips printed on the front, and I overheard her telling friends the lips were from a movie called *Rocky Horror* which her sister went to see every weekend. The only other thing I recall from the conversation I'd eavesdropped on was the mention that the film only played late at night, and my classmate with the shirt wasn't allowed to attend with her older sibling.

I had no idea at the time what Rocky Horror was, but the idea of a movie playing in a theater late at night did something to me and put me on a mission that consumed my mind like nothing else up to that point in my young life.

When I arrived home from school that day, I rummaged through a stack of old newspapers my dad kept by the back door and found a copy of the previous Friday's edition. Sure enough, *The Rocky Horror Picture Show* was listed as playing at a local theater called The Fox Twin at midnight on Friday and Saturday in Theater One, while Theater Two featured bloopers and uncut scenes from episodes of the Little Rascals and Three Stooges films. This was the same theater where I had seen features such as *The Towering Inferno* and *Earthquake* (both released in 1974) with my dad, and *Star Wars* (1977) with nearly every kid from my neighborhood. A similar midnight program was happening across town at the Jerry Lewis Cinema.

My young heart raced.

How was I going to get my strict parents to let me go to these late-night films? Were any of my older cousins going to them? Were any of my friends' older siblings attending? I knew this was going to continually gnaw at me, and for a few years, it did.

But in the meantime, I managed to find out everything I could about The Rocky Horror Picture Show, most of which came from word of mouth through cousins and an older neighbor. I became insanely jealous of those able to not only attend midnight screenings of the film, but those who were part of its legendary floor show and audience participation. And while I couldn't wait to see the film at my local Staten Island theater, when I learned what was going on up in Manhattan at the 8th Street Playhouse, time pretty much came to a standstill for me. From the moment I found out about midnight movies around 1978-79 until my freshman year of high school, I was obsessed. In 1980, I found a book at my local bookstore called THE OFFICIAL ROCKY HORROR PICTURE SHOW MOVIE NOVEL (1980 A&W Visual Library), which featured actual, chronological stills from the film, and featured the dialogue and song lyrics in cartoon bubbles, making it a "real-life" comic book-like version of the film. I must've read through it 100 times while listening to the soundtrack album during my junior high years. At long last, my first midnight screening happened just before Christmas of 1982 during my freshman year of high school. I managed to pull the old "I'm sleeping at my friend's house" routine but left out the detail we'd also be attending Rocky Horror. In the pre-internet days, there were no advanced ticket sales, so my friend and I kept our fingers crossed we'd not only be admitted to the R rated feature, but that the show wouldn't be sold out. The Rocky Horror Picture Show, which had moved from the Fox Twin across town to the Island Twin, wasn't drawing the crowd it once did, at least on Staten Island. We were admitted into the R rated film with no questions asked but were surprised to see only 15-20 people in attendance. Thankfully, many of them knew the lines to shout back at the screen, and my first midnight movie experience turned out to be better than it looked like it was going to be.

But I knew I had to somehow get up to 8th Street and experience the film the way it was meant to be seen. Just a few months into 1983, with my parents now a bit more lenient with me staying out later, my friend and I attended our first Rocky Horror screening at the 8th Street Playhouse and to say I was blown away would be a gross understatement. Following 90 minutes of pre-movie shenanigans (which could take up its own chapter of this book), the film finally started at 1:30 a.m. and by the time it all ended I had become mesmerized. There was simply nothing else like this happening in any other theater (at least, that's what I thought until I learned of the film's worldwide fandom which I read about shortly after this screening in Bill Henkin's incredible THE ROCKY HORROR PICTURE SHOW BOOK (1979 Dutton Adult), which somehow alluded me until a friend's older brother let me borrow his copy). I attended Rocky Horror a total of 60 times at the Island Twin between 1982-1985 and caught a wild screening during the summer of 1983 in New Jersey at a theater called the Cinema Alley. During those three years, I also returned to 8th Street for a couple more screenings. I met some people at the Island Twin, and we eventually created our own little floor show, but something else was brewing in the theater next door that began to grab my attention.The Island Twin featured Rocky Horror every Friday and Saturday at midnight in Theater One, but also another midnight movie every weekend in Theater Two, and never the same film. Between the years of 1983-1986, I attended midnight screenings of *Dawn of the Dead, Pink Floyd The Wall, The Exorcist, Day of the Dead, ReAnimator, A Clockwork Orange,* and *Night of the Living Dead.* There was also a concert film titled *Urgh: A Music War!* that featured a barrage of new wave and punk bands that turned me on to lots of music I'd never heard before. I'd often attend *Rocky Horror* on Friday, but toward the end of my time as a Rocky fanatic I found myself looking more forward to the film that I'd be seeing next door on Saturday. The Island Twin screened some of their mainstream fare at midnight, too, and I attended a couple of those offerings, but there's a time for certain films to play, and the midnight hour simply isn't for the latest entry in the Star Wars series. Each week I'd religiously obtain a copy of the Village Voice, which featured what I considered not only the most insightful film reviews around, but the most comprehensive listing of screenings in and around New York City. The 8th Street Playhouse, for quite a while, offered midnight movies *every night of the week*, always headed by the Friday and Saturday Rocky Horror screenings. 8th Street's attractive ad in each issue of the Voice made me drool: among its ever-changing midnight roster was *A Clockwork Orange, Pink Floyd The Wall, Blood Feast, The Gore Gore Girls, Apocalypse Now, The Song Remains the Same, Andy Warhol's Bad, El Topo, Pink Flamingos, Ralph Bashki's Wizards, Videodrome, Elevator Girls in Bondage* (yes, you read that last title correctly) and seemingly countless others. The theater itself was just a wonderful place, where I also enjoyed screenings of other cult films such as *Repo Man, Morons from Outer Space* and *The Decline of the Western Civilization Part 2: The Metal Years* during regular hours.

Just a few blocks south, at the Waverly Twin (which has been renamed the *IFC Center* since 2005), early 80s midnight screenings of local horror classic *Basket Case* and slasher hit *The Slumber Party Massacre* were favorites with late night crowds, as well as the sci-fi mind-bender *Liquid Sky.* I had the pleasure of attending the kooky horror comedy *I Was a Teenage Zombie* there for its 1987 midnight premiere, as well as the fun splatter-fest *Street Trash* and nutjob Troma sequel *The Class of Nuke 'Em High 2: Subhumanoid Meltdown.* A haven for midnight films since the mid-70s when they were the first place to hold screenings of *Rocky Horror*, the Waverly/IFC Center continues to be one of Manhattan's best bets for consistent midnight fare. The Bleecker Street Cinema also offered a good midnight selection, and among my favorites there were the midnight premiere of *Frankenhooker* and a retro midnight screening of *The Harder They Come.* In 1985, *The Toxic Avenger* became a hit with midnight crowds there and played every weekend for almost an entire year. Between the non-Rocky Horror screenings at the Island Twin, as well as 8th Street and the Waverly, I quickly learned that while Rocky Horror was considered the king of midnight movies, it certainly wasn't the only one, nor was it the first to have fans line up to see it week after week (which, thanks to Samuels' book, I had already been informed about). I'm sure I'm not the only one who came into the midnight movie fold thanks to Rocky Horror, and for that I'll always be grateful. But the midnight movie world goes far deeper than doing the time warp and throwing rice and toilet paper at a movie screen. It *is* important to note, however, that Rocky Horror has continued to play at one theater or another in Manhattan since 1976. I revisited the film in December of 2019 at the Cinepolis Chelsea Cinemas in midtown Manhattan where descendants of the 8th Street Playhouse keep the famous floor show going alive and, I am glad to report, very well. It continues to play once or twice a month to sold out crowds at another downtown Manhattan theater, albeit with a 10:00 p.m. start time.

Theaters such as the Angelika Film Center, where I had seen *Henry, Portrait of a Serial Killer* in 1989 shortly after they opened, also kept midnight movies going throughout most of the 1990s.

I had been out of the midnight movie scene for a while, beginning in the early 1990s, due mainly to raising two kids and my (then) new job which required getting up at a ridiculously early hour. I still attended films during normal hours and continued to read the Village Voice almost every week. Around 1997 when I started using the Internet with the rest of the world, I visited movie theater websites to see what was playing at midnight. It seemed midnight screenings, while still there, had greatly slowed down.

It wasn't until June of 2008 when my love for midnight movies could no longer contain itself. I saw an ad in the Voice for a film titled *Mother of Tears,* which was the long-awaited third part to Dario Argento's *Suspiria/Inferno/* Three Mothers trilogy, and it just happened to be playing only at midnight engagements in Manhattan at the Landmark Sunshine theater. It was my first midnight film since 1991. And whatever you may think about the campy Suspiria sequel, I loved every minute of it, and I loved every minute of my time back in the theater at the witching hour. The Sunshine featured midnight movies every weekend until finally closing its doors in 2018, and during those ten glorious years when I had got back in the saddle, I was able to see midnight screenings of, among others, *Doctor Butcher MD, Zombie, The Warriors, Dawn of the Dead, Pink Flamingos, The Theater Bizarre, Eraserhead, Gone with the Pope* (if you haven't seen the trailer for this lost gem do so immediately) and the incredible *All About Evil,* which featured a live pre-show to rival anything seen in Rocky Horror during its 8th Street days. I also attended a midnight screening of *The Room,* which featured an incredibly lively Rocky Horror-like amount of audience participation.

It wasn't long after my *Mother of Tears* screening when I started getting back into more regular midnight shows, thanks in large part to not only the Sunshine but the IFC Center. In late 2009, early 2010, I finally got to see classics such as *El Topo* a few times as well as Jodorowsky's next film, *The Holy Mountain,* which I've now seen at midnight over a dozen times. And since then, the list of midnight movies I've seen at the IFC Center has been amazing: *White Dog, A Clockwork Orange, Eraserhead, Cruising,* as well as newer fare such as *The Human Centipede 2: Full Sequence* (which featured one of the liveliest crowds I've ever been a part of) and it's less than stellar third chapter, *The Human Centipede: Final Sequence.*

INTO THE REEMERGENCE: Since 2010, a trio of theaters across the river in Brooklyn began to feature regular midnight screenings each weekend and helped contribute to what I believe has been a reemergence of midnight movies. All three are found in Williamsburg, the most popular of them being the Nitehawk Cinema, where I think I've seen more midnight movies in ten years than I'd seen anywhere else beforehand. *Blue Velvet, Mulholland Drive, Possession (1981), Cannibal Ferox, Silent Night, Bloody Night (1972), The Sentinel, Fascination (1979), Urgh! A Music War, Blood Feast, Switchblade Sisters, New Year's Evil, Repo Man, Without a Stitch (*see my review this issue), and so many more it's nearly impossible to remember despite having saved most of my ticket stubs (and sadly, over the past few years, physical, printed out ticket stubs have been going away thanks to online ticketing. Some of us film geeks aren't happy about it). Many of their films are screened the old-fashioned way, in glorious 35mm, and crowds are often lively and enthusiastic. It was great to once again catch another midnight theatrical screening of *Urgh! A Music War*, only this time there were some fun pre-film music videos added as a bonus. In fact, before any screening at the Nitehawk, a 30-minute pre-show of shorts and oddities related to the main feature are often shown, so if you ever plan on attending make sure to arrive early. The pre-show for a midnight *Blue Velvet* screening I attended was worth the price of admission on its own. A few blocks away is a tiny store-front cinema run by volunteers called the Spectacle Theater, who feature unusual films every day of the week, and two different midnight films each weekend. Among the gems I've seen there are *Nekromantik, Last House on Dead End Street, Schraam, Love Me Deadly,* and probably oddest of all, a 1986 kiddie film titled *Hawk Jones* about a young boy who declares war on crime in his neighborhood (it worked very well as a midnight feature for reasons I'm still trying to figure out). Films are screened from a laptop directly behind the back row, and you're welcome to bring your own refreshments. A fun if slightly uncomfortable theater, their midnight programming is kind of incredible, as is their schedule during regular hours, and on rare occasions they feature 16mm screenings. The place has the feel of a real 70s grindhouse, complete with a bathroom that's accessed on the side of the screen! Incredible. Not too far from the Spectacle is the Film Noir Cinema, who for a while featured midnight fare. Among some of their late-night offerings have been *Alucarda, Don't Deliver us from Evil,* and *The House that Jack Built.* Pretty much run by one man, the front of this place is a still-active DVD rental store, but walk to the back and you'll enter a small movie theater with a decent sized screen. They advertise screenings often at the last minute, and I find myself checking their website all the time to see what's scheduled for the next (or same) day. While their midnight schedule has vanished since Covid, hopefully it will return sooner rather than later. Yet another Williamsburg theater/bar called Videology featured some solid midnight films, but since Covid the place has turned into a stand-up comedy club.In March of 2020, the Covid pandemic shut down most theaters in NYC, and midnight movies came to a screeching halt. But thankfully in the summer of 2021, midnight screenings slowly started to return, and as of September 2021, it was good to see the Spectacle bring their midnight program back. The Nitehawk restarted its midnight program in October 2021, as did the IFC Center. While most of the films I've enjoyed at midnight since 2008 haven't been what you'd call "midnight movies" in the sense they play week after week, most of them have been unusual, unique, and simply not suitable for mainstream audiences or regular screening hours. Midnight movies *should* be unusual and not appealing to the average movie goer, which is why I couldn't understand the IFC Center's midnight screenings of films such as *Jaws, Ghostbusters,* and *Jurassic Park.* But, hey, if *The Holy Mountain* or *Eraserhead* are simultaneously playing in their other theaters, all's still right with the world. (It should be noted that some midnight screenings of *Ghostbusters* at the IFC Center featured a full Rocky Horror-like cosplay cast running around the theater, circa 2018).

(This article is an excerpt from Nick Cato's forthcoming book, MIDNIGHT MOVIES: BEYOND THE 1970-1982 GOLDEN ERA AND THE 2010 REEMERGENCE)

(* "Ben Barenholtz, Midnight-Movie Innovator, Is Dead at 83" by Richard Sandomir in the New York Times, 7/5/19)

Released in 1968 in Denmark under its original title, **UDEN EN TRAEVL**, softcore sex comedy **WITHOUT A STITCH** came to America in December 1969, and played on Broadway in NYC, then seedier theaters and drive-ins until 1975. As far as I can find, it hasn't played American theaters since then. But on Friday, July 3, 2015, the wonderful Nitehawk Cinema in Brooklyn, NY hosted a rare 35mm screening of this once controversial film*, which was based on the 1966 novel by Jens Bjorneboe.

The beautiful Anne Grete Nissen stars as Lillian, a teenager ("I'm 17 and a half!") who fears she might be frigid. Her sort-of boyfriend Henry can't please her (even after they go to his parent-free house) and a lesbian encounter (of sorts) with her friend Lise has her questioning everything. Lise suggests she go see a sex therapist, and the opening section of the film takes place in the office of Dr. Petersen, a gynecologist with some very unusual methods (especially for a 1968 film).

It takes a bit, but Petersen manages to bring Lillian to orgasm (there's plenty of unintentionally hilarious dialogue here, most of which had the Nitehawk Cinema in stitches) and suggests that she "doesn't rely on him" for future fulfillment: "You can't keep experiencing pleasure at the expense of Blue Cross!" He recommends she travel around Europe and keep a diary of her experiences. I had to laugh at this point because:

a) it seems 90% of all "erotic foreign cinema" has this same plot and b) I couldn't stop thinking about the episode of SEINFELD where George Costanza rented a film titled RACHELLE, RACHELLE, that had this same story line.

But moving along ...

Lillian soon finds herself hitchhiking across Sweden, where she meets a cameraman. They have sex in his small truck then he convinces her to star in one of the porno films he's shooting. In these scenes, and most scenes after, Lillian hears the teachings of Dr. Petersen in her head whenever she doubts trying something new. I have a feeling this slap in the face of traditional morals made the film more controversial than the nudity and sex scenes themselves. Just about everything Dr. Petersen says to Lillian in the opening office sequences goes against every Puritanical teaching known to man!

When Lillian hits Germany, she enters a huge restaurant/beer hall. As she sits and listens to the conversation going on around her, a large Oom-pah band takes the stage to wild applause from the audience. I don't know what it is about this scene, but it had me laughing my ass off, and wanting to drink a mug of Dinkleacker. Lillian meets a man who invites her over to his home, and it turns out he's rich. A butler serves them dinner, and when they go to his bedroom, he breaks out a whip. Again, Lillian hears the words of Dr. Petersen, and endures the beating (although it's more playful than brutal). And just when you thought this guy was a complete prick, he offers the whip to Lillian. Let's hear it for equal opportunity sadists! I haven't seen FIFTY SHADES OF GREY, but I'll bet anything this brief sequence is more entertaining than the entire film (and book series).

For some reason, the Danish language, subtitled film becomes English when Lillian arrives in Italy. She meets a handsome gent who we eventually learn is gay, but to be kind to tourists, he invites Lillian to join himself and his boyfriend in one of the strangest (and shortest) threesomes ever committed to celluloid. In fact, this quick scene is hilarious as it attempts to show the tryst artistically. And in another threesome (sorry, can't recall what country this takes place in), Lillian and a lady friend first partake in an incredibly strange yet traditional dance number before they get down to business.

As funny as WITHOUT A STITCH is at times, I found it a more bizarre offering than a sexual one. Besides the overall anarchist/hedonistic tone, who knew mud wrestling was so popular in 1968? And the mud wrestling sequence here (at a club, I believe, while we're still in Germany) is simply off the wall, as the two competitors both look like wardens from a women's prison film. Lillian and the crowd are splashed with mud as they cheer them on.

There are a couple of truly disturbing scenes throughout the film, one being where boyfriend Henry, frustrated over Lillian's teasing and inability to be pleased, comes after her with a fireplace poker! But thankfully he tosses it aside and tries once again to satisfy her.

(Anne Grete Nissen stars as Lillian in WITHOUT A STITCH, enjoying German beer as an Oom-pah band rocks out)

After her sexual odyssey, Lillian returns to Dr. Petersen, and he's thrilled to hear his suggestion worked. She's now cured and ready for action, although she really needs to do something about that gigantic, overgrown ... you get the picture.

WITHOUT A STITCH is a real time capsule of a film. While it was surely a letdown for moviegoers seeking more of the nasty stuff, this soft-core outing is hilarious and strange as it breaks taboos few other films did at the time ... at least films that could be seen in major theaters. There are so many funny lines, you'd be wise to watch with a pad in hand to remember half of them, and kudos to director Annelise Meineche for actually shooting the film in Sweden, Germany, Denmark, and Italy (and probably a couple more).

In 1973 a sequel titled BETWEEN THE SHEETS hit foreign theaters but didn't come to the U.S. until the video days. No one from the original was involved, although it was shot in Denmark.

Star Anne Grete Nissen was only in two more films (1970's BEDROOM MAZURKA and 1971's DAGMAR'S HOT PANTS, INC.), but judging from this slice of vintage euro trash her acting abilities wouldn't have carried her much further.

As the film's tagline proclaimed, "You've never seen anything like this before!" And for 1968, you pretty much hadn't.

(* WITHOUT A STITCH was a popular international hit, and one of the first films to feature a young woman enjoying sexual adventures, hence the controversy.)

"Cato's debut novel **Don of the Dead** is insanely entertaining – a splattery, whacked-out novel with outrageous characters and a frenzied pace. Miss this one, and you might as well be wearing cement shoes while zombies eat your face."

– *Jeff Strand, author of The Sinister Mr. Corpse and Pressure*

2024 edition now available on Amazon

Satan in the 70s:
OCCULT CINEMA EXPLOSION

Between ROSEMARY'S BABY (1968) and Hal Lindsey's bestseller THE LATE GREAT PLANET EARTH (1970), America, and most of the world, had become obsessed with the Antichrist. While Satanic cinema had been brewing since the dawn of film itself, biblical prophecy, thanks to Lindsey's book, pushed Satan and the end times into the mainstream like never before. Is it any wonder that both Hollywood and indie filmmakers went absolutely *insane* during the 70s with occult and devil-themed films? When I was 4 or 5 years old circa 1973, I received as a gift a 3-minute silent film on Super 8 titled EQUINOX, which featured all the film's stop motion monster scenes, and while I had already been a Godzilla and Universal monster fan, this short film (that I wouldn't see in its entirety until the VHS days) lured my impressionable young ass into the world of occult cinema.

Here are some of the best (and not so best, yet still fun to watch) occult films of the 1970s...

EQUINOX (1970). This stop-motion monster-filled low budget romp features an "occult barrier" being opened after an ancient tome is tampered with (basically a pre-cursor to 1982's THE EVIL DEAD). In fact, EVIL DEAD's plot is nearly identical to EQUINOX: four college students go into the woods looking for their professor. They find his isolated house has been destroyed and his copy of the Necronomicon missing. Raimi's film, although low-budget, features much better creature effects, acting, and is genuinely scary, whereas EQUINOX's cheesy stop-motion monsters and shady acting make the film work today as a "so-bad-it's-good" camp classic. *But it came first.*

After finding their professor's house destroyed, the students encounter a forest ranger who turns out to be a demon god in human form. The students find a cave where a strange old man gives them a book he claims holds magical powers. When the park ranger learns of this, he sends all types of creatures after them to retrieve it. And it's these creatures that make EQUINOX such an enjoyable film to watch: one ape-like beast with blue fur looks like something from a SINBAD film, while an oversized caveman complete with club provides questioning laughs. The crème de la crème is a flying, horned demon and a gigantic specter that generates some solid thrills.

Our students discover the magical book, the Necronomicon, has opened an "occult barrier between good and evil," as proclaimed by the film's attractive poster, unleashing these monsters into our world.

The film's lone survivor, Dave, resides in a mental hospital, and the film is told through flashbacks as he recalls the ordeal in the woods. The giant specter told him he'd die in a year upon his escape and closing of the portal. His friend Susan — whom he presumed died with the other two students — visits him in the hospital at the film's conclusion. Dave goes completely insane after seeing her wicked-looking face, and we're left to assume the demon who had possessed the park ranger now resides in Susan.

EQUINOX was obviously a project to show off the stop-motion monster skills of the special effects team, and the results, while amateurish, are highly entertaining. It should be noted that visual effects artist Dennis Muren went on to win Oscars for his work on STAR WARS (1977) and JURASSIC PARK (1993).

While the possessed park ranger isn't exactly scary-looking, he carries a certain dark aura that works well among the cast of nobodies (although one student is played by Frank Bonner, who would find fame eight years later as sales manager Herbert "Herb" Tarlek on the TV series WKRP in Cincinnati).

A fun monster romp that doesn't feature anything graphic, EQUINOX is one of the few films in this subgenre that is family-friendly despite its occult themes. The film was released theatrically around Halloween of 1970, and then showed up on VHS in the mid-1980s under the title THE BEAST. The latest release was a beautiful deluxe double-DVD set released in 2006 by the Criterion Collection.

BLOOD ON SATAN'S CLAW (1971), a British folk horror classic which takes viewers back to the early 18th century, when pagan practitioners – and those unjustly accused of witchcraft – were tortured and killed. The theme of the film is similar to that of its folk horror successor, THE WICKER MAN: Ancient beliefs and witchcraft lead to Satan worship or other harmful behaviors.

Like many folk horror films, pagan rituals are used as a cautionary tale. Films like this are unique to British and Scottish Isles and removing them from that setting is detrimental to the story (see the dreadful 2006 remake of THE WICKER MAN). The collision of the old ways of the Druids and the pious ways of the Church of England makes for great drama.

(Linda Hayden as the sinister Angel Blake, jumping another member into her devil cult in THE BLOOD ON SATAN'S CLAW)

Younger members of a small town become fascinated by a deformed skull, which is discovered on a piece of farmland. After they start growing furry patches of skin, they become convinced the skull is from someone who was possessed, and they also find a claw they believe was part of the discovered remains. Before long, ringleader Angel Blake starts recruiting the rest of the town's kids in an abandoned church. Rituals and creepiness abound. They're attempting to rebuild the demon corpse body, but of course the adults are doing all they can to put a stop to this outrageous devilry.

Considered one of the three classics of the folk horror genre, CLAW is a wonderfully shot film that holds up great to repeat viewings. In 2023, screenwriter Robert Wynne-Simmons, after all these years, wrote a novelization of the film, and to my delight it is *fantastic.*

***

Starting out as a drive-in favorite, then a staple of late-night TV, **THE BROTHERHOOD OF SATAN** (1971) is a prime example of low-budget horror done right. In some ways, the film is superior to the slickest Hollywood releases.

The first time I "saw" BROTHERHOOD, I actually listened to it. I was around eight years old, and my parents were watching it after my bedtime on Monday night movie. I had no idea what was going on, only that my dad mentioned someone had just chopped off someone else's head, and there were a bunch of devil worshippers kidnapping kids and killing their parents. Naturally, when VCRs became popular in the early 80s, THE BROTHERHOOD OF SATAN was one of the first films I sought.

The film begins with a family trying to escape their small town when they see a young boy in the middle of the road playing with a toy tank. They attempt to drive around him but end up off the road stuck on a slight hill. Suddenly, a regular-sized tank appears and crushes the family to death inside their station wagon. Before the opening credits roll, we see the young boy walking away from the scene with his toy tank, causing casual movie viewers to scratch their heads and fans of the weird to settle in.

This isn't going to be your typical horror flick.

Ben and his new girlfriend Nicky (played by Ahna Capri from 1978's PIRANHA) are on their way to celebrate his eight-year-old daughter K.T.'s birthday at his mother's house (K.T. is played by Geri Reischel, who looked much older just a year later in the horrible I DISMEMBER MAMA). Before they arrive at the party, they come across the accident scene, and go to get help. They end up in the town of Hillsboro, to which the family tried to escape, and soon learn no one can get in or out of the town.

But how were they able to get in?

THE BROTHERHOOD OF SATAN then becomes a surreal puzzle of a film, as Ben and Co. slowly discover what's happening around them.

There's a coven of elderly witches in town. They're just about to conduct a ritual that promises to restore their youth, and guess who they're eyeing as the final child for their dark purposes?

Despite an abundance of clues and information Father Jack finds in some old witchcraft books he had saved, Sherriff Pete plays the dumb small-town cop a bit too dumb, forcing the priest and Ben to take things into their own hands when K.T. goes missing.

What makes BROTHERHOOD work so well is the character of Doc Duncan, the leader of the coven. Portrayed by Strother Martin (who would later star in the 1974 snake thriller SSSSSSS), he comes off as a happy, loving grandfather type you'd trust to babysit your children. As the town's doctor, he's generally liked by everyone. The mere thought that an ordinary guy can have such a wicked double life gets eerier the more you let it sink in.

While the first half of the film moves slowly, it keeps you in suspense and allows countless ideas to come to mind about just what's happening. And by the time the non-Satanist adults realize what's going on, it's too late to do anything about it, giving BROTHERHOOD one of the darkest and strangest endings of all 70s horror films.

Smarter than your average drive-in fare and stranger than most cult films, THE BROTHERHOOD OF SATAN is a real treat for horror fans tired of the same old thing, even all these years later.

THE DEVILS (1971). Ken Russel's controversial epic about a cardinal in 17th century France who is accused of witchcraft and corrupting a convent of nuns. While the "possession" here is handed off as mass hysteria, the film easily falls into the "nunsploitation" category and is unforgettable no matter how you look at it.

In plague-infested 17th century France, Cardinal Richelieu (played by an amazing Christopher Logue) convinces Louis XIII they need to destroy wall-protected cities throughout the country to prevent the spread of Protestantism. He has his eye on the city of Loudun, where a priest (Father Grandier, played by Oliver Reed) has taken charge in the wake of their governor's death. Father Grandier is loved by most and is a faithful minister, but he's also having sex with another priest's daughter and harbors other secret sins.

Meanwhile, Sister Jeanne (Vanessa Redgrave), the head of a local convent is in lust with Grandier, and when she learns he has secretly married, she goes insane and tells his sins to another priest. She also accuses Grandier of witchcraft and causing her to become possessed.

(Vanessa Redgrave leads a convent of hysterical nuns in Ken Russell's incredible THE DEVILS)

This leads to the arrival of an off-balanced exorcist and two helpers who try (often hilariously) to exorcise Sister Jeanne and her entire convent in one of the wildest exorcism sequences ever filmed. Father Grandier is eventually found guilty of witchcraft — even though being innocent — and is burned at the stake.

Despite the possessions being faked and the cause of mass hysteria, THE DEVILS' use of sacrilegious imagery and infamous censored sequences makes it of note to occult cinema fans, not to mention the masterful directing of Ken Russell. Technically this is an artistic, dramatic view of an historic event and not an occult film, yet it fits in perfectly with films such as MARK OF THE DEVIL (1970) and INQUISITION (1976). I was fortunate enough to see a 35mm print of this at the Alamo Drafthouse in Brooklyn in 2017. Don't hesitate to see this on a big screen if you get the opportunity.

ASYLUM OF SATAN (1972) Director William Girdler (who would later direct the successful JAWS-like GRIZZLY (1976) and

1978's THE MANITOU) delivers this cheap but effective first effort set in a mysterious insane asylum.

Lucina, a lovely concert pianist, is taken from a regular hospital, where she was being treated for exhaustion, to the Pleasant Hill Sanitarium. When she wakes, she has no idea why she has been transferred and demands to speak with her regular doctor. But she is assured her doctor arranged this, so she reluctantly agrees to their treatment, even though she swears there's nothing wrong with her.

When Lucina finally meets her doctor, it's hard not to laugh at his goatee and devilish eyebrows. We already know he has something sinister in store, despite his friendly way of handling Lucina's concerns.

One night Lucina hears noise in the room above hers, so she decides to check it out. She discovers a chair rocking on its own right before being attacked by a one-eyed zombie-looking thing. She escapes, and we're never told what this thing was and why she was able to so easily escape it.

As Lucina adjusts to sanitarium life, which consists of being locked in her room when not being treated, her fiancé Chris is doing all he can to locate her after learning she has gone missing from the general hospital. He finds out she's been taken to Pleasant Hill, and when he investigates, Doctor Spector (gotta love that name) tells him visitors are not allowed as it may interfere with the patients' treatments.

Chris brings a detective back only to find the place boarded up, but he sneaks back later and discovers the place is up and running and apparently up to no good. Chris is played by Nick Jolley, a painfully unattractive man who dresses in the epitome of horrible 70s fashion, which doesn't enhance his mutton chops. You must give the guy credit for risking it all to find his woman.

As Chris investigates, we learn Doctor Spector is older than he looks and is also involved with immortality experiments. He uses bugs, snakes, fire, and an unidentified gas to "treat," torture, and eventually kill his patients.

But he has other plans for Lucina. His treatments were nothing more than priming rituals to ready her as an offering to Satan in exchange for more years of life. She's brought to the basement dressed in a virgin-white gown and placed on an altar. Hooded worshippers surround the table when Martine enters and recites some satanic passages. When she's done, she peels off her face to reveal she's actually Doctor Spector (big shock here). A puff of smoke comes before him as Satan enters the room. The devil mask used here is one of the phoniest I've ever seen in a film, and according to one article I read, the body suit was originally used in ROSEMARY'S BABY.

Despite all ASYLUM's goofiness, it should be noted this is one of the first horror films where not being a virgin works in someone's favor. Thanks to a flashback scene of Lucina and Chris, we know she's not a virgin, and apparently so does Satan. He rejects her as Doctor Spector's offering and burns him to death.

When Lucina is rescued by Chris and a small police force, she is in the asylum's abandoned basement. Was this all a figment of her imagination or was there really a Doctor Spector? We learn it was all real when Chris stays behind after Lucina is taken outside; he sees Satan and his followers as we get a close-up of him screaming.

He meets Lucina outside, and we're left to wonder if he's now possessed, a question that will never be answered as there was no sequel and director Girdler passed away in a tragic helicopter accident in 1978.

ASYLUM OF SATAN is a cheap, horribly acted film but for a first feature has its merits. Some scenes are genuinely spooky, and star Carla Borelli delivers a decent performance as Lucina. She went on to star in Days of Our Lives, Falcon Crest, and several TV shows in the 70s and 80s. Much of the film is unintentionally funny, yet there's a genuine sense of worry from the moment Lucina wakes early in the film that keeps us interested and concerned.

I'd highly recommend this for fans of hooded-cultist films and those who like really, really, really bad-looking monster masks.

(Christopher Lee as Lord Summer Isle in THE WICKER MAN, arguably one of the greatest (and smartest) horror films of all time)

THE WICKER MAN (1973). A police sergeant investigating a missing child on a Scottish isle meets his fate at the hands of local pagans. Not only one of the best occult horror films of all time, but one of the best FILMS of all time. If you've never seen it make sure to see the "Final Cut," released in 2013 to theaters and Blu-ray, which is the version that should have been released from the get-go (Christopher Lee's character comes off twice as sinister). Unforgettable, essential viewing.

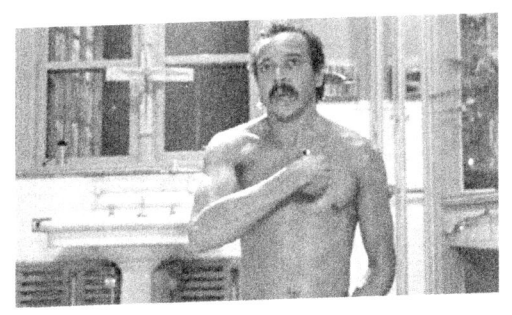

(Bill Gunn both directs and plays a crucial role in his 1973 masterpiece, GANJA & HESS)

GANJA & HESS (1973) Instead of taking the money and making a typical "blaxploitation" film, director Bill Gunn created this brilliant art house horror head-scratcher about a man who becomes addicted to blood after being cut by an ancient, germ-infested knife (and no, this is *not* a vampire film). Worthy of multiple viewings, NIGHT OF THE LIVING DEAD's Duane Jones stars alongside genre favorite Marlene Clark in this rare gem of a movie. I have a lengthy article about this film in my book *Suburban Grindhouse*, but suffice it to say it's easily one of the most unique offerings from the 70s, blending a religious and occult storyline into something never before seen on screen.

MESSIAH OF EVIL (1973). A genuinely underrated classic if there ever was one. A woman is searching for her artist father in a coastal California town when she runs afoul of a zombie-like Lovecraftian cult. One sequence inside a movie theater is as intense as it gets. Great atmosphere and oddly original. See last issue for a look at the recently released Radiance box set.

In the UK-lensed **PSYCHOMANIA** (1973), Tom Lathan (played by British stage actor Nicky Henson) is the leader of a biker gang called The Living Dead. They hang around a cemetery that surrounds a circle of Stonehenge-like rocks local legend claims were seven witches who broke a deal with the devil.

Tom is fascinated with the idea of "coming back" from the other side. He tries to talk about this with his girlfriend Abby but gets distracted when a large frog comes across their path. He stuffs the frog in his jacket to bring it home.

Tom lives in a lavish mansion with his mother and her butler, Shadwell, who is played by legendary actor George Sanders in his final film role.

Tom's mother is a medium and is giving a séance just before he arrives home one evening. He asks her for the key to a room that's been locked for 18 years, the same number of years his father has been dead. He believes the room holds the secret to returning from the dead. With nudging from Shadwell, she agrees to give him the key and tells her son he might find the secret "depending on who you are."

His mother teaches him that the key to overcoming the afterlife is to truly believe you will come back at the moment of death. She explains that Tom's father lost faith in the final seconds and wasn't able to return.

Tom is determined.

He tells the rest of The Living Dead about this and decides to be the example. While speeding down a roadway, Tom drives his motorcycle off a bridge and dies. Abby gets permission from his mother to bury him in their cemetery hangout, and she agrees. They bury him sitting on his bike, and Shadwell even shows up to toss a frog-amulet into the grave with him.

All is quiet, until a couple's car breaks down near the cemetery. The husband reluctantly cuts through it to get help, and it's at this moment we hear Tom's motorcycle revving up underground. He bursts from the earth, runs over the man who was passing through, and meets up with his gang.

Thinking he is kidding, one member tries to stab him in the back, but it has no affect. "You can only die once," Tom says, and convinces the rest of the gang to commit suicide and join him to truly live up to their name.

Out of the eight members, seven kill themselves, and only one lost faith at the last moment and doesn't return. The last to join them is Abby, but Tom isn't convinced she killed herself.

PSYCHOMANIA is full of kitsch and dark humor, but it also has an eerie style all its own, and a soundtrack that, while a staple of the time period, adds a certain post-mod element that's hard to pinpoint. Some of the scenes have a surreal edge, and of course with its post-hippie clothes and hairstyles, there's a psychedelic aura all around.

Despite some video companies labeling it as such, PSYCHOMANIA is not a zombie film. Tom and his gang return from the dead looking, talking, and acting the same as before they died, albeit with super-strength and a bigger thirst to cause trouble. One of the female members even runs over a baby in its carriage inside a supermarket, although nothing is graphically shown. They aren't flesh eaters or Romero-zombies. They are bikers with an occultic leader who taught them how to conquer death. The Living Dead here are like dark versions of the Messiah, pictures of deceived antichrists who don't realize their time back on earth is extremely limited.

Although PSYCHOMANIA is readily available on DVD and even to watch for free online, seek out the special edition Severin Films DVD release from 2010, which features a beautiful transfer of the film and exclusive, new interviews with several of the film's stars. This flick used to be on TV nearly every weekend when I was a kid, and I lost track of the number of times I've sat through it.

Quite possibly one of the most beautiful, challenging, and eerie of all 1970s occult films, Mario Bava's **LISA AND THE DEVIL** (1974) is unlike any film that came before it.

While on a tour of Spain, Lisa (played by the gorgeous Elke Sommer) leaves her group when a strange antique shop catches her attention. The store is full of unique items. As she browses, she meets a man named Leandro (the always suave Telly Savalas) who has purchased a mannequin and the same carousel she considered purchasing. Leandro is a dead ringer for a mural portrait of the Devil she saw on her way to the shop. Alarmed, Lisa runs from the shop, only to knock into a man who had been following her, sending him down a flight of stone steps to his death.

Now on the verge of panic, she can't find her tour group but manages to meet up with a wealthy couple who agree to give her a ride to her hotel. On their way over, the couple's car breaks down by an old mansion where Leandro is employed as the butler.

The couple attempts to get Leandro to let them stay as their chauffer works on the car. He reluctantly agrees, but Lisa once again becomes creeped out by Leandro and flees. On her way out, she meets up with Maximillian, the son of the countess who owns the mansion. He convinces his mother to let them stay.

This is where LISA AND THE DEVIL becomes a real brain-twister. The man Lisa had knocked to his death is now stalking her again, peeking in windows with his ghostly visage. Lisa learns this man is Carlos, the countess's second husband. She overhears him, Maximillian, the countess, and Leandro discussing that she is actually named Elena, Maximillian's old girlfriend, a woman the countess never liked.

Lisa doesn't know any of these people, and she has a wild dream about her supposed past, concluding with Carlos's morphing into the dummy she saw Leandro purchasing at the beginning of the film.

Back to reality (or is it?), the chauffer is killed while he works on the car. The husband who drove Lisa to the mansion demands his wife leave with him, but she ends up running him over and is murdered herself by Maximillian.

The film then becomes stranger yet as Leandro dresses Lisa up as he claims Elena dressed. As he does so in a room full of mannequins, he explains to Lisa how he is a demon in service to the countess and Maximillian. He explains the mansion is cursed and exists for all who are in it to relive their deaths over and over. The mannequins represent each person.

(The great Telly Savalas stars as the Devil ... or does he?)

The countess begins to go mad, and Lisa and Maximillian want to leave, but Maximillian has a sudden change of heart when he sees Lisa as Elena. He takes Lisa to a secret room, and we discover Elena's corpse is housed within.

Maximillian goes crazy. He drugs Lisa and rapes her, but Elena's ghost interrupts him, causing him to run downstairs and confess his murderous ways to his mother. His world closes in around him as his victims come forth in an unsettling sequence, which ends with Maximillian jumping out a window to escape and finding himself impaled on the business end of a sharp metal fence.

The film's finale must be watched repeatedly to grasp. Lisa wakes up in the empty mansion and tries to flee. She comes across a mannequin of Maximillian who tries to convince her to stay with him. She easily escapes and gets back into town where she meets up with Leandro who is refusing to take a doll of Elena the antique shop owner offers him. Leandro doesn't take the doll as Lisa makes a beeline for her plane.

Once onboard, she walks around to discover she's the only living person on it. The other passengers are the dead bodies of everyone she met in the countess's mansion.

She runs to the cockpit to alert the pilot only to find the pilot is Leandro.

Lisa passes out and becomes Elena's mannequin from the mansion. The film ends with Leandro walking off holding it.

LISA AND THE DEVIL is a film that requires a few viewings. At first, it's frustrating, but the puzzle becomes clearer the more you look at everything through the eyes of Leandro and not Lisa. We end up believing Leandro is either the Devil himself or at least the demon he claimed to be.

Many people first saw this film under the title THE HOUSE OF EXORCISM, which was LISA AND THE DEVIL with some exorcism scenes thrown in to cash in on the success of THE EXORCIST. Kino Lorber Video released a special edition DVD that contains both cuts of the film, but one need not to waste their time on THE HOUSE OF EXORCISM.

LISA AND THE DEVIL is arguably Mario Bava's greatest achievement and is easily one of the smartest horror films of all time, not the "occult gobbledygook" one reviewer proclaimed.

In **ABBY** (1974), William Marshall (yes, BLACULA himself) plays Garnet Williams, an archeologist who's also a bishop.

While on a trip to Africa he unleashes a sexually perverse demon that follows him back to America. The demon possesses his daughter-in-law, Abby, played by the fantastic Carol Speed, who uses more swear words here than Joe Pesci in GOODFELLAS (1990). William and Abby are members of the same church, and this demon's apparent goal is to bring the place down.

Abby lives a normal life, but it takes a plunge as soon as this demon enters her. Upon moving into a new home, she abuses her minister husband Emmett, makes fun of the size of his penis, assaults a pastor at her church, grows an incredible sexual appetite, and gets horny over the sight of chicken blood. She spews all kinds of profanity and vomit and wanders off into the city right after Garnett returns home to exorcise her.

Garnett, Emmett, and Abby's brother Cass, who happens to be a cop, search for her before she can harm anyone else or herself.

ABBY was shot for the insanely low budget of $200,000, and at times you can't help but laugh at the absurdity of it all. Thanks in large part to Speed's performance, the film works despite the fact it's THE EXORCIST for the Blaxploitation set. There's some genuinely eerie atmosphere especially when the demon is first unleashed in an African cave, and at times Speed's demeanor really makes us question if she's just acting or the actual host for one horny demon. Some might think I'm crazy to say this, but try watching it alone, in an empty house, after midnight. This thing *works*.

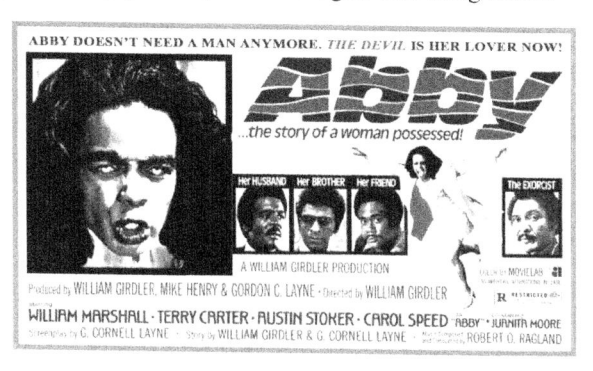

I understand it may be hard for some people to take this film seriously. After all, there's a scene in which Abby scares a white woman to death (!) and there are plenty of black stereotypes, including an abundance of fried-chicken eating. Even so, it's worth a viewing, especially for the exorcism/possession sequences that rival and surpass similar films with much larger budgets. After all, what else are you watching an EXORCIST rip-off for?

Italy's **THE ANTICHRIST** (1974) is one of those films with about a dozen other titles (upon its 1978 American release, it was **THE TEMPTER**), but whatever name you see it under, it's quite a grim experience.

Carla Gravina delivers an incredible performance as Ippolita, a handicapped and sexually frustrated thirty-something woman who develops serious mental issues after her mother passes away in the car accident that paralyzed her. She looks like a cross between Amanda Plummer and Mia Farrow in ROSEMARY'S BABY (1968) but with a more sinister grin.

Ippolita lives with her family (including her father, played by genre great Mel Ferrer), who cares for her. Confined to a wheelchair, she attends a religious healing service to no avail. She sees some guy cursing at a statue in the church, and he eventually kills himself by jumping off a nearby cliff. When Ippolita arrives home from the service, her father is kissing a woman, and it freaks her out. She worries he'll remarry and no longer take care of her. She acts nasty and goes on anti-God rants to their family priest.

Upset with her behavior, Ippolita's father hires a psychiatrist who discovers through hypnosis that Ippolita was a witch in a past life burned at the stake for worshipping Satan. Once this is brought forth, it somehow causes Ippolita to "fall back" to her past life.

(Carla Gravina as Ippolita in THE ANTICHRIST. Sure, it's another EXORCIST rip-off, but three times as fun)

She falls asleep the same night her past life was revealed and finds herself in an orgy in Hell. Uncut versions of the film feature Ippolita giving oral sex to a goat. This is when THE ANTICHRIST becomes an off-the-wall, sex-charged horror film. After this wild dream, she gets out of her wheelchair, jumps on her family's dinner table, and asks all of them to have sex with her in a demonic voice.

Now fully possessed, Ippolita can walk again, and her first stop is a museum where she meets and seduces a young man, then kills him by twisting his head around 180 degrees. Then the other standard EXORCIST happenings occur: Ippolita becomes uglier in each scene, her language worsens, and almost every time we see her, objects float around the room. At the conclusion, an old-school Catholic exorcist arrives to begin the exorcism.

THE ANTICHRIST's first half still manages to shock, from its use of bestiality to Ippolita's sexual conduct. The way she attempts to seduce her own brother brings the creeps full throttle, and a sequence where she makes some poor guy eat green vomit from her hand could make the most jaded devil-film fan gag.

As far as blatant EXORCIST clones go, THE ANTICHRIST is one of the best, but that doesn't mean it's flawless. Far from it, in fact. But thanks to Gravina's unforgettable performance, and a director (Alberto De Martino) who wasn't afraid to offend anyone, it's a solid, underrated gem of Euro-horror that gets better with each viewing.

The late Carla Gravina won a best supporting actor award in 1980 at the Cannes Film Festival for the film LA TERRAZZA. I knew she had the goods!

ALUCARDA (1975) This Mexican film, directed by Juan Lopez Moctezuma, who had previously produced, and partially filmed Alejandro Jodorowsky's famous midnight cult hit EL TOPO as well as his earlier effort, FANDO AND LIS, is a real gem of both possession and nunsploitation cinema. With powerful performances, disturbing images, and a real sense of dread throughout, whatever cheesiness that comes through is quickly forgotten.

The film opens with a woman giving birth and praying that God will save her young soul. The baby turns out to be the title character, Alucarda, who is taken to a convent by the midwife. Actress Tina Romero plays Alucarda as well as the woman who gives birth to her in this opening sequence.

We flash forward and meet a girl named Justine, who arrives at the convent after the death of her parents. She befriends Alucarda, and Alucarda falls in love with her a bit too quickly. Justine goes along with things, being the new girl in town.

One day they frolic through the woods surrounding their convent and come across a group of gypsies, one of whom looks like a comical version of a satyr/Satan. When they leave, they find a cave filled with tombs. Unknown to them, this is also the cave in which Alucarda was born.

Letting her dark curiosity get the best of her, Alucarda opens one of the tombs and becomes possessed. She makes Justine worship Satan along with her and is bent on making a blood pact that will seal them together forever.

In one of many "what-the-hell's-going-on" moments, Alucarda and Justine find themselves in the middle of a gypsy orgy, and while it's not clear if something possesses Justine, the experience changes her life.

Back at the convent, Alucarda and Justine make trouble during class, and their nun-teacher accuses them of blasphemy. In an attempt to purge this evil out of the convent, the nuns flog themselves while a meeting with a local doctor convinces the Mother Superior that Alucarda and Justine need a good old-fashioned exorcism.

The rest of ALUCARDA is complete mayhem, with blood flowing like water, more screaming than has ever been heard in any other film (no joke!), and one of the eeriest convent worship sanctuaries I've ever seen. One scene of Alucarda and Justine visited by the satyr-like male gypsy is as beautiful as it is disturbing.

(Tina Romero and Susana Kamini are the ultimate scream queens in ALUCARDA)

What sets this one apart from other nunsploitation films (besides the mummy-like habits they wear) is Alucarda herself. From the moment we meet her, it's apparent she's the outcast, dressed head-to-toe in black (I guess Mexican convents allow freedom of dress?) and always questioning everything around her just by her stares. After her possession, she becomes a hybrid of a demon and a vampire and seems bent not on destroying her convent——but converting it. We hate her, we love her, and are never sure if we want her to be cured or continue with her satanic lunacy.

Another key character who gives the film a real kick is head priest Father Lazaro, who commits himself to getting the devil out of Alucarda and the whole convent with absolute zeal. He even attempts a dual exorcism and has the nuns tie Alucarda and Justine to two crosses inside the sanctuary in one of the film's most memorable sequences. Father Lazaro was played by David Silva, a famous Mexican actor who made his final film appearance here after starring in over 120 films since the 1930s. Man, *what a way to go out!*

The film's soundtrack is unique, too, in that it blends gothic organ music with some dark psychedelic backing tunes, giving the whole thing a sound that's as bizarre and creepy as the images they support.

ALUCARDA is by no means a perfect film, especially with its dialogue that at times gets overdramatic and downright silly. But actresses Tina Romero and Susana Kamini take their roles seriously, and even when they're spewing forth goofy evil rants, we don't know if we should laugh or hide behind the couch. You'll probably be doing both. Don't let this small flaw fool you: ALUCARDA is hardcore underground 70s horror at its finest and most gruesome. It's filmed on an art house level at most times and isn't afraid to bash the Catholic Church or the viewer right in the face with its barrage of sex, violence, and blasphemy.

If you've never seen a nunsploitation film before, this is arguably the ultimate example of the subgenre next to Ken Russell's THE DEVILS (1971). You may want to bathe in holy water before viewing just to be safe.

THE DEVIL'S RAIN (1975). You just can't get more 70s than this: William Shatner battles devil cult leader Corbis (Ernest Borgnine) in a rural town. It's a slow burner but is creepy as it gets and is capped off by a dual shock ending. Church of Satan leader Anton

LaVey was supposedly flown in for guidance during the ritual sequences. I wonder if he got to hang with (victim) John Travolta?

Although there were many before it, THE DEVIL'S RAIN became a template for "hooded Satanist" films. With sacrifices, occult rituals, and massive Satanic imagery, it isn't too hard to see why the film has a dedicated cult (pun intended) following. In 1975, upon the film's release, a relentless TV ad campaign ran all night long, featuring glimpses of the film's infamous "meltdown" finale.

Perhaps even more intriguing than the all-star cast are the behind-the-scenes rumors. Reportedly, so many odd incidents happened during production that Ernest Borgnine (this issue's cover model) refused to appear in this type of film again. But his role as Satanic cult leader Corbis has become iconic and arguably the symbol of all 70s occult horror films.

Despite some over acting from William Shatner (what a shock there!), THE DEVIL'S RAIN is serious business. This isn't a fast-paced film, but unlike similar slower films it gets under your skin. The sense of dread spills off the screen in nearly every sequence.

RACE WITH THE DEVIL (1975). Buddies Peter Fonda and Warren Oates take their ladies on a trip in an SUV. But after witnessing a satanic ritual murder, they're chased from Texas to Colorado by pissed off devil worshipers in this action-heavy horror flick with a genuinely shocking ending. A hybrid of 70s devil worship *and* road movies, Fonda fits perfectly here right off his iconic role in EASY RIDER, and some of the chase sequences are downright exciting.

And remember, folks: if you ever witness a satanic ritual while you're out in the desert on vacation, keep in mind that even devil worshippers have jacked up trucks and motorcycles. BEWARE…

***

Quite possibly the epitome of a so-bad-it's-good film, **SATAN'S CHEERLEADERS** (1977) is a horror comedy from Greydon Clark, who directed the cult classics BLACK SHAMPOO (1976) and JOYSTICKS (1983) among many others. But this mixture of devil film and teen comedy is insanely entertaining and cemented Clark's reputation as one of the finest exploitation filmmakers of all time.

The film opens on a beach with a bunch of high school students playing touch football as some of the school's staff watches. It's really goofy stuff followed by typical comedic hijinks back at their school. These scenes take up about half of the film's running time, but we do discover the school's janitor, who spies on the girls in the shower, is involved with a satanic cult and has his eyes on our four cheerleaders, Debbie, Patti, Sharon, and Chris. We can't forget their names as they're written across their cheerleading uniforms' skimpy T-shirts.

(Before becoming a bunch of satanic witches, SATAN'S CHEERLEADERS didn't exactly behave like Sunday school students)

Jack Kruschen plays the janitor named Billy Brooks, who looks like a cross between Wilford Brimley and Uncle Jessie from The Dukes of Hazard. He projects a creepy-but-cartoonish aura whenever he's onscreen. After this first section of CHEERLEADERS unfolds (complete with some porn-sounding background music), Billy decides it's time to go after our girls as his coven seeks a human sacrifice.

The girls are driving their van to an out-of-town game when they get a flat tire. Mr. Brooks just happens to be driving by and gives the girls a lift, but he drives them to an isolated section of the woods. He puts some kind of spell on Patti through a quick and questionably filmed ritual by a well, turning her into a witch. Or something.

Brooks passes out from the ceremony, and the girls hightail it out of there and wind up at the house of the local sheriff and his wife (played by John Ireland and Yvonne DeCarlo of *The Munsters*).

They turn out to be the head of a town full of Satanists who eye Patti for their human sacrifice (and surprise, surprise -- John Carradine shows up as a homeless man who tries to warn the girls about the weird local population). Little do they know Patti has been granted powers of her own thanks to Mr. Brooks.

The girls try to escape the town, get thwarted by the cult, and make another escape attempt until they at last overcome.

Dobermans seem to be the satanic dog of choice (at least in 70s and 80s horror cinema), and we get two of them here running all over the place. At one time they're sent after the cheerleaders, only to be scared off by Patti's newfound magic.

SATAN'S CHEERLEADERS is chockfull of ridiculous, brain-numbing dialogue, atrocious special effects, and arguably the dumbest group of protagonists you're likely to see in a film. The humor level never gets above Scooby Doo quality and the mild sex talk and quick glimpses of skin barely make this an R-rated feature. Its original trailer claimed this was rated PG. It takes a while to get going, but when it does there's just something about it that miraculously works, albeit in a campy, bad-movie sort of way. Amazingly, I first saw this at 10:00 am one Saturday morning in 1980 on a local TV station, where it played regularly.

(Witches get a major upgrade in Dario Argento's SUSPIRIA)

SUSPIRIA (1977). Highlighted by Goblin's incredible (and incredibly scary) soundtrack, Dario Argento's masterpiece about a dance student whose new ballet academy turns out to be the front for a witch's coven is one of the most beautifully shot horror films ever made. Occult horror blends with giallo-type murders into an unforgettable artistic nightmare. Kudos to Udo Kier and one vicious dog for their unforgettable cameos.

(I found the 2018 remake incredibly tedious (many like it more than the original for some reason). The overlong film does boast a wild final 30 minutes (preceded by two hours of boredom), but it'll never top the original).

Based on Jeffrey Konvitz's 1974 novel of the same name, **THE SENTINEL** (1977) has become a cult favorite over the years due mainly to its cast of popular actors. Konvitz co-wrote the screenplay, and comparisons to the famed novel are quite close despite the film not working half as well as the book.

Rumors say the film was originally a made-for-TV project (it does feel like one during the opening credits), but the official theatrical release date was Jan. 7, 1977 in New York City where it received mixed reviews from critics and fans alike. Die-hard horror fans know Italian horror-film master Lucio Fulci was inspired by this for his classic THE BEYOND (1981), but newcomers should be aware that THE SENTINEL is not an all-out gore-fest.

Fashion model Alison Parker (played by Cristina Raines) is dating lawyer Mike Lerman (Chris Sarandon) who keeps haunting her to marry him. She wants to be on her own for the time being and rents an apartment in a Brooklyn Heights brownstone facing lower Manhattan.

She learns that a blind priest named Father Halliran (played by the legendary John Carradine) lives on the top floor and is the only other person residing in the building. The weirdness begins when she starts meeting neighbors her landlady didn't tell her about, including the goofy Charles Chazen (an over-the-top but great Burgess Meredith) and a lesbian couple who provide some funny and awkward dialogue. There's also VACATION (1983) star Beverly D'Angelo as the kinky Sandra who masturbates while having a conversation with Alison in a truly disturbing sequence that goes on for a bit too long.

(You'll never watch VACATION the same way again after seeing Beverly D'Angelo in one of the most uncomfortably disturbing scenes of the 70s)

When Alison complains about her strange neighbors to the landlady, she is told she must be imagining things.

The film gets weirder still: Alison has a flashback/dream of a suicide attempt and goes to investigate noises upstairs where she witnesses a ghoul-like man in the upstairs apartment with two spooky-looking naked women lying in the bedroom. When he tries to get her to join their hellish orgy, she stabs him, cuts his nose off, and runs outside where she collapses on the street. Her boyfriend Michael is among the crowd that finds her, and in a neurotic state she claims she just killed her *father*.

THE SENTINEL suffers from some slow moments, but we learn this brownstone is inhabited by a group of excommunicated Catholic priests, and Father Halliran sits watch on the top floor as the place also happens to be a gateway to Hell.

The film caused some controversy upon its initial release when it was learned the producers used deformed people to portray the demons who attack Alison during the finale. Even if THE SENTINEL had a budget five times larger than it did, I doubt they could have pulled off the final demonic assault described in Konvitz's novel, so perhaps this was the easiest way to get a jolt out of the audience. Either way, the scene works until Father Halliran shows up with his large cross and stops their attempt to leave the building.

In the "shock" ending, Alison sits in Father Halliran's apartment, overlooking Manhattan; she is the new sentinel, her destiny now fulfilled.

Like so many occult films of the 70s, THE SENTINEL is one full of flaws, yet it manages to work and actually scare at times. The aforementioned sequence of Alison's encounter with her ghoul-father is considered one of the scariest horror film moments of all time among many genre fans, and its ROSEMARY'S BABY-like atmosphere when the neighbors show up manages to keep the viewer on edge.

The film sports an almost endless array of cult actors, including Ava Gardner, Arthur Kennedy, Christopher Walken (as a detective in a wasted side-plot), Eli Wallach, Jerry Orbach, Jose Ferrer, and Hank Garrett. There are so many cameos you can play a drinking game: take a shot whenever a new star appears. You'll be blitzed before the film is halfway over.

The first novel I ever read as a kid was Konvitz's *The Sentinel*. While it's still a much better time than the film, I do appreciate the fact Konvitz had a big hand in the screenplay and that he also wrote a seldom-read sequel in 1979 titled *The Guardian* that happens to feature one of the darkest endings of all time.

THE SENTINEL is a few steps above a "so-bad-it's-good" film in that it's sure to give you a few genuine scares and implant several images that won't leave your psyche anytime soon.

(Why an order of Vatican Bishops chose/destined a NYC fashion model to be the new guardian of the gates of hell is anyone's guess. And just why is one of the gates of hell in downtown Brooklyn? Just go with it...)

FILMS BLURAYS STREAMING THEATRICAL SCREENINGS

LAMB (2021) is another film I was bored to tears with for the first half of its running time but was glad I stuck it out. This is a demented Icelandic folk fairy tale, with several WTF-moments and a grim finale. I'm sorry I didn't see it on the big screen as the cinematography is fantastic. This is kind of like PADDINGTON BEAR on seven hits of Swedish acid.

CONTRABAND (1980) is Lucio Fulci's dive into the poliziotteschi genre, featuring Fabio Testi smuggling cigarettes and booze into Naples via speedboats and pissing off local gangsters. There's a scene that rips off Sonny's death in THE GODFATHER, and being a Fulci film, there's plenty of over-the-top gore (for a gangster film). Cauldron Films released a Blu-ray in 2022 and it's probably still streaming on Tubi. You'll love it.

(Renzo Palmer goes super-psycho in THE BIG RACKET after thugs rape his daughter)

THE BIG RACKET (1976): Enzo G. Castellari (of 1990: THE BRONX WARRIORS fame) directs this rogue cop / poliziotteschi epic starring Fabio Testi as Inspector Nico Palmieri, who is continually shot down by his bosses and an annoying lawyer as he attempts to save a small community from an extortion gang. After he's fired for getting too involved, Palmieri gathers a team of former criminals (and one dad/ restaurant owner hell-bent on revenge after his teenage daughter is raped by said gang). One member is a famous skeet shooter, who also helps Palmieri out earlier in the film. Palmieri finds out the gang is going to be present at a meeting of local mob bosses at an isolated factory and manage to get there a day early to plan their attack, which goes down in wonderfully violent fashion featuring endless shoot-outs, dynamite action, and Palmieri managing to get not one, not two, but three cars to explode using only his mighty handgun. Renzo Palmer is great here as the restaurant owner, who goes from timid nerd to killer of jailhouse rapists to street executioner. His transformation steals the show from star Testi, although Testi is fine here as the pissed off Inspector who takes down the mob, literally losing his shit in the final seconds of this superior euro-crime thriller.

THE COMMUNE (2009) is a well-made independent film. It deals with Jenny, the child of divorced parents, who spends the summer of her 16th birthday at her father's neo-hippie new age commune (she looks about 25, but we'll let that slide). From an early scene of Jenny dancing around her room to the pagan imagery seen all over the compound, it's apparent director Elisabeth Fies was heavily inspired by THE WICKER MAN. There's some decent tension throughout, dark family secrets, and a couple of sequences that go on for about double the length they should have. Yet despite the familiarity of the whole thing, THE COMMUNE works. It's a decent homage to the occult horror films of the 70s. Director Fies really put her all into this (she even does the only female nude scene), and it's worth a look for those who want to see a ROSEMARY'S BABY meets WICKER MAN-hybrid done right. While I didn't buy most of the hippies/pagans living in the compound (I found most of them comical), I thought Stuart G. Bennet did a fine job as Jenny's father/cult leader Dr. Polieos, and lead actress Chauntal Lewis does a decent job (even if she looked 9 years older than her character).

A decent time killer that works much better than the other, way overrated 2009 psuedo-70s/80s flick, THE HOUSE OF THE DEVIL.

***

If you're one of those film-goers who HATES really, really, really bad cinema, you might as well skip this review of **ANOTHER SON**

OF SAM (1977). But if you enjoy inept filmmaking, horrendous 70s fashions, plot-holes galore, and a *genuine* grindhouse experience, pay attention: For the first 5-6 minutes of this 74-minute epic, we see a cop walking around a dock with his girlfriend and then water skiing. I still have no idea why, but that's the least of this film's puzzles. Next, we're treated to some local North Carolina lounge singer named Johnny Charro, who sings as our cop relaxes with his girl after a long day's water skiing. Again, I have no idea why.

ANOTHER SON OF SAM

Around 15 minutes in, the film finally begins: A psycho named Harvey (and nope--the name has nothing to do with the dog that allegedly told the real Son of Sam to kill) is injected with sedatives at a mental institution. But apparently, they shot him up with steroids. Harvey kills two orderlies and a nurse, then escapes to a local park where he kills two cops as a dozen others run in circles looking for him.

Before long, Harvey finds his way to a state college where he hides in a girls' dorm room, eventually taking two of them hostage, despite the fact the cops evacuated everyone from the building (the two girls miraculously show up in their room after they had left the campus and the place had been quarantined--one of many questions not worth asking or worrying about).

Despite the fact a SWAT team is called in, the local cops are still running all over the dorm trying to locate the elusive killer, who is shown in BLOOD FEAST-style eyeball close-ups (and on occassion we see his moccasins tip-toeing down hallways). We eventually learn Harvey had been sexually abused by his mother as a child, so the cops call her in to try and talk her son out of the hostage situation. It works, giving our cops and SWAT-sters time to blow a couple dozen holes in him.

ANOTHER SON OF SAM is crudely edited, poorly lit, features fashions that will make even 70s fans glad the decade is long gone, music that sounds like left-overs from an HG Lewis film, and best of all, poster art that's better than the film itself. As a show of total *classlessness*, this film was released in 1977, before there was any other fictional film about the Son of Sam, and (I'm assuming) while Berkowitz was still at large. Shot with the working title HOSTAGES, the producer went above and beyond to re-title his film in a way that might possibly draw a crowd and make him some moolah (I'm not sure if it did either). Speaking of said producer, North Carolina local David Adams also wrote and directed and cast and edited this seldom-seen gem of pure trash--- PLUS he was a stunt coordinator (being a former stunt man himself). If you like your films trashy, pointless, and full of unintentional laughs, ANOTHER SON OF SAM is pure gold. All others, turn and run away as *fast as you can*. I had discovered this through Something Weird Video's download offerings.

(A barely recognizable Nic Cage is fantastic in LONGLEGS)

LONGLEGS (2024): After a year of an impressively mysterious trailer/ad campaign, and some high-praising reviews, LONGLEGS was unleashed to theaters on July 12, 2024, and it did not disappoint. It's basically a satanic version of THE SILENCE OF THE LAMBS, with Nicolas Cage as a doll-making-occult serial killer (who, despite starring in 6 films a year, is fantastic here and easily deserves a best actor nod at the Oscars) and Maika Monroe of IT FOLLOWS plays FBI agent Lee Harker, although unlike Clarice from LAMBS, she has a partial-psychic ability to pinpoint places serial killer Long Legs has struck. Harker's mother is played by Alicia Witt and ends up being a demented scene stealer.

The whole cast does a fine job, the film looks fantastic (it's set in the 90s, but could pass for a retro 70s feature), and the entire mood and tone are downright creepy. I'm looking forward to director Osgood Perkins' next feature, THE MONKEY.

BLACK ROSES (1988): Continuing with the heavy metal cheese he started a year earlier in ROCK 'N' ROLL NIGHTMARE (which starred campy heavy metal body builder Thor), late director John Fasano delivered this batshit crazy look at Satan working through a super-lame heavy metal band to test their powers on a small town before embarking on a world tour. And while I watched this once as a VHS rental, on July 10, 2024, a screening was held at Brooklyn heavy metal bar Lucky 13, hosted by the Brooklyn Horror Society and the Troma Team, hence creating the perfect setting for a revisit.

(11 years before starring in THE SOPRANOS, Vincent "Big Pussy" Pastore gets whacked by a speaker demon in BLACK ROSES)

BLACK ROSES is classic 80s exploitation: devil worship, high school students who look like they're in their 30s, clueless adult characters, body doubles for some nude scenes, fun puppet/monster FX, and most baffling of all is some of the cast: I'd love to know how legendary drummer Carmine Appice was conned into this project: he plays the drummer of our possessed band, and his real band (at the time), King Kobra, supplies most of the soundtrack.

Second, the legendary Julie Adams of THE CREATURE FROM THE BLACK LAGOON fame appears as one of the uptight parents, and Carla Ferrigno plays the ex-wife of our hero English teacher (she's the sister of Lou (HULK) Ferrigno). A psychotronic cast if there ever was one, the audience cheered in glee when Vincent Pastore ("Big Pussy" from THE SOPRANOS) shows up as a stereotypical Italian parent of one of our high school students, only to get eaten and sucked into a blaring speaker by a spider demon! Band leader Damian (!) is played by stage actor Sal Viviano, who has the terrible acting chops to front this terrible, clichéd band (and if you think he's bad here, his next project with the same director, THE JITTERS (1989), proves acting just wasn't his calling). I understand the director was a metalhead, but, sorry folks, the stuff this band plays is corny, *commercial hard rock,* which gives BLACK ROSES a super cheesy feel anytime the band is playing one of their ridiculously embarrassing songs. Even back in the 80s I remember scratching my head over how fucking atrocious this music was (which breaks my heart as a drummer, as Vinny Appice once played the cans for proto-metal band CACTUS, not to mention for OZZY during his 1983 *Bark at the Moon* tour).

A so-bad-it's-good time, especially with a lively crowd such as the one I saw it with at Lucky 13, BLACK ROSES is strictly for fans of campy low budget horror and metalheads who, for whatever reason, want to hear some of the worst "metal" ever recorded.

***

Sushi Typhoon (Japan's answer to Troma Films) unleashed another manga-inspired sci-fi/action/splatter/slapstick dark comedy titled **YAKUZA WEAPON** (2011), which I first saw at the 10th annual Asian Film Festival in NYC, and am happy to report it still holds up great. Like MACHINE GIRL, this one deals with a gang lord who is enhanced after being captured by the government...this time with a machine gun arm (that turns back to a human arm at will) and a rocket-launcher hidden in his new flip-down knee!

But our anti-hero Shozo (played with comic glee by Tak Sakaguchi) was a lunatic even before his amputated body became weapon-enhanced. After serving 4 years in the jungle (I'm assuming with the military?), Shozo returns home to Tokyo to find his father (a mob kingpin) murdered and his family's hang out turned into a seedy "loan" store. When Shozo learns a rival gang leader is trying to take over the entire underworld by shooting up various gangs with a new "hyperdrug," all hell breaks loose. With only a few brief scenes of a tame nature, YAKUZA WEAPON is an almost constant barrage of kung-fu action, gunplay, sword fights, and some really off-the-wall sequences (Shozo's pissed-off girlfriend welcomes him and his 2 friends home by tossing a small speed boat at them, almost crippling him!).

(Actor, director, (literal) street fighter, and all-around bad ass Tak Sakaguchi stars in the insane YAKUZA WEAPON)

The highlight of the film features Shozo up against a naked female robot who fires mini-missiles from her vagina (!) and her head flips down to unleash some serious machine gun fire (yes—the Japanese know how to party!). There's also a 4-minute fight scene that was filmed in *a single take*, yet it looks as if it were professionally choreographed.

Co-Director Yudai Yamaguchi has gone ballistic to see that his fans have a good time, and he has succeeded quite well. Kudos to co-director and star Tak Sakaguchi, who played a major part with the fight scenes here.

With gallons upon gallons of blood (although some of the CGI-splatter looks a bit silly), heads and limbs flying all over the place, and as much old-school fist/foot fighting as any classic karate film, YAKUZA WEAPON is one of the more entertaining Asian mob flicks to come down the pike in years.

MAXXXINE (2024) closes Ti West's "Maxine" trilogy, and while I enjoyed this well enough, **X** remains my favorite of the director's string of retro-slasher films. This time, Maxine is in LA, now a semi-famous porn star, who manages to nail an audition for an upcoming horror film. But as she attempts to move her career into "regular' movies, her porn colleagues are being murdered, obviously by some kind of satanic cult who know about her deeds (from the previous film). There are some gruesome kills, a couple of good-looking nods to classic giallo films (including a killer in black gloves and hat), and one painful sequence where the term "ball-buster" is taken to an extreme new level. My main gripe is one of the detectives, played by Bobby Cannavale. I'm a big fan of his, and here his character is way too comical, making him come off as a throw away side note. Kevin Bacon, however, is great as a sleazy PI, who meets the most gruesome demise in the film. Giancarlo Esposito is a real scene-stealer as Maxine's bad ass agent/porn producer. Mia Goth, once again, isn't anything remarkable. I thought she was great in PEARL (oddly my least favorite of the series), but I'm convinced she's the most overrated of the current crop of Hollywood scream queens.

(Merissa Mell and Antonio Sabato become lovers in GANG WAR IN MILAN, a sub-par, yet entertaining effort from Umberto Lenzi)

GANG WAR IN MILAN (1973) is another euro crime thriller by the great Umberto Lenzi, but nowhere near as good as his classic THE TOUGH ONES (aka ROME, ARMED TO THE TEETH). This time, Antonio Sabato plays a Sicilian pimp who runs a legit produce service for cover and goes up against a French heroin dealer bent on becoming partners. Sabato, as Salvatore "Toto" Cangemi, isn't believable here, coming off more as a lounge singer than a ruthless gangster, but thankfully, actor Alessandro Sperli saves the day as Billy Barone, a tough as nails, cigar-chomping OG just back from Chicago, who helps Toto and the Frenchman come to terms … before double crosses and the obligatory shit starts hitting the fan.

Jasmine Sanders (played by Merissa Mell of DANGER: DIABOLIK and SATAN'S WIFE (see review last issue)) is good as the femme fatale with a secret (who refers to Toto as "Sicily"), and Antonio Casagrande is great as Toto's right hand man Lino, who survives a testicular torture that will have most guys grabbing their junk (or the fast forward button). Nowhere near as good as the similarly titled GANG WAR IN NAPLES, this WAR is for euro crime completists only (and for anyone who wants to see a hooker get drowned in an octopus tank…)

FROM CORLEONE TO BROOKLYN (1979) is Umberto Lenzi's final poliziotteschi film, this time starring the great Maurizio Merli at Lt. Giorgio Berni, who must transport mob witness Scalia from Italy to New York City to testify against a mafia boss named Barressi. It's pretty much a hybrid of THE GODFATHER and THE GAUNTLET, as Berni and Scalia face all kind of assassination attempts at every turn on their international road trip. There are plenty of shoot outs, fights, and some unintentionally funny dialogue, all the things that make euro crime so damn good. Barressi is played by Mario Merola, who starred in a ton of Italian gangster films from the early 70s up until 1981's THE MAFIA TRIANGLE. He's great as a don who enters the US using a fake south American passport (!). Sonia Viviani (who was also in Lenzi's NIGHTMARE CITY) has a small role, and several thugs are played by extras from Fulci's ZOMBIE (you won't recognize any of them).

Despite Merli throwing punches this time and not his trademark man-slaps, this is a fine flick shot in both Italy and the US, where Lenzi obviously had a blast filming a sequence where Berni and Scalia take a cab through Times Square (see following pics).

(Some great views of the Victory Theater and other marquess (including two different theaters showing THE WARRIORS) are a nice surprise for vintage marquee-addicts in FROM CORLEONE TO BROOKLYN)

SHE IS CONANN (2023): Director Bertrand Mandinco's 3rd film has a similar feel as his 2nd, AFTER BLUE (2021, which was like a modern EL TOPO), yet quickly comes into its own weird world and I believe is his finest feature yet.

This is a surreal, feminist take on Conan the Barbarian, and while some fans of Robert Howard's original stories may take offense, I think if they stick around for the third act they'll be as enthralled as this old school Conan/Howard fan was.

Like the comic KING CONAN, an elderly barbarian queen tells the story of her life since she was forced into savagery as a teenager right up to her last bizarre incarnation. It seems every ten years or so, Conann becomes a completely different person, with a different persona, played by different actresses. In her 40s, she becomes a Nazi-like warlord in an obvious tribute to THE NIGHT PORTER and the ILSA films. But it's the aforementioned third act when Conann, now pushing 60, is a rich Matriarch who offers her fortune to a group of artists if they'll perform one demented act, an act which brings both LA GRANDE BOUFFE and THE HOLY MOUNTAIN (both 1973) to mind.

(The dog-faced Rainer leads Conann through her psychedelic odyssey in SHE IS CONANN)

SHE IS CONANN may wear its influences on its sleeve, but somehow Mandinco manages to deliver a unique, authentic vision that would've easily been a midnight cult film had it been released in the 1970s. The perpetually foggy and glitter-filled sets and constant droning background sound give this the feel of a post-apocalyptic nightmare, yet we never know exactly where we are: hell? A planet such as AFTER BLUE? Purgatory? The barbarian queen's own damaged mind?

My favorite part of this twisted journey is Rainer, a dog-faced cerebus-like mutant who guides Conann through her incarnations and continually snaps photos to document everything. He's played by Elina Löwensohn (from SHINDLER'S LIST), walking around in a studded leather jacket with long hair and his name printed on the back like a rockstar (I'll assume the name Rainer is a tribute to Fassbinder?).

With lots of stylized violence, twisted dialogue, great practical effects, and a dream-like aura that's all its own, any fan of unusual cinema should be in their glory during this epic that's like a Moebius comic strip from HEAVY METAL magazine come to life.

THE HEROIN BUSTERS (1977) is another euro crime thriller from Enzo G. Castellari, released just a year after THE BIG RACKET, with Fabio Testi (looking like Rick Springfield in the 'Jessie's Girl' video) as an undercover cop trying to thwart an international drug distribution ring. His boss is played by the great David Hemmings (of THIRST (1979) fame), who, in order to keep the cover, must act like he believes Fabio is an actual thug (the scenes of them fighting in front of the other cops are hilarious). Sherry Buchanan (from DOCTOR BUTCHER, MD) has a brief role as a junkie, and you'll recognize most of the bad guys from other Italian horror/police films. Bonus points for the finale, in which Fabio chases the head drug dealer in a small one-man plane, giving things the feel of a small-scale 007 flick. Fun stuff. An abandoned spaghetti factory was used for one of the shootout scenes. Mama mia!

THE OLD ONES (2024) is director Chad Ferrin's follow up to his 2020 Lovecraftian THE DEEP ONES, and while I haven't seen it, I can say his latest is an atrocious combination of several Lovecraft stories that's beyond bad. Just because a feature boasts it has "practical special effects" doesn't mean it's a good film, or that it has good effects. Most of the creatures here are little more than masks purchased at a Spirit Halloween store sale, and one sequence of a shoggoth attacking a guy in a toilet stall is so unconvincing it's not even laughable: the creature looks like a shittier version of THE BOOGENS (1981), something I thought would never be possible. With mostly junior high-level acting and a finale that will have both Lovecraft and Stuart Gordon vomiting in their graves, THE OLD ONES is pure garbage from start to finish, and I'll assume all the unwarranted positive reviews I've seen online are written by friends of the director. Kelli Maroney has a pointless cameo, and star Robert Miano, while okay here in the lead, is nowhere near as memorable as he was way back when in DONNIE BRASCO.

TRAP (2024) is the latest by M Night Shyamalan, a director who has always been hit or miss with me (and most people), and here he delivers a major league miss. Josh Hartnett is very good as serial killer Cooper, trying to find his way out of a sold-out concert where police have set a trap to get him, but that's where the fun ends. The concert is performed by "Lady Raven" who is played by the director's daughter Saleka, so this was obviously a multimillion dollar attempt to promote her musical career. So much screen time features her concert footage any viewer will become weary, and I doubt even fans of pop music will like these lame songs. TRAP also features countless plot holes, making it obvious not another soul edited, commented on, or even read Shyamalan's script. The whole thing plays out like an ABC movie of the week. The final act is beyond frustrating, and there's no twist ending (something fans of the director have come to expect). What we do get is a *dumb* ending, especially when it is revealed how the police and FBI knew the killer was going to be at the concert in the first place. Despite Hartnett delivering a fine performance, save yourself some aggravation and re-watch him in the far superior 30 DAYS OF NIGHT (2007). I'm absolutely done with Shyamalan. And, yes, if you change the **T** to a **C** you'll get the proper title for this forgettable flick.

On August 10th, 2024, I attended a 50th anniversary screening of **THE TEXAS CHAINSAW MASSACRE** (1974) at the Museum of Modern Art in NYC. The film ran daily for a week, but unfortunately I couldn't get tickets for the opening night festivities which included a Q&A session with star Teri McMinn, screenwriter Kim Henkel, cinematographer Daniel Pearl, and production manager Ron Bozman. However, not only was it great to once again see my all-time favorite horror film on the big screen (my first time was during a 1981 re-release), there was plenty of interesting reactions during the screening: One elderly woman passed out after Franklin had his arm cut in the van (I'm not sure if this was due to the film or if she forgot to take her meds), three others walked out within the first 40 minutes, and during the infamous dinner sequence, two millennial guys left, clearly offended/disturbed. This film is *50 years old* and still freaking out and upsetting people. That is ART, my friends. And judging by these theatrical reactions, it makes me wonder if some of the younger generation of "fans" will at some point try to have certain films banned. Were these two gents who left after an hour into the film *that* offended at Marilyn Burns' iconic performance? Are they going to start proclaiming films such as *Chainsaw* have no place in the modern world? Time will tell. And in the meantime, perhaps some of us should get ready to defend the films we have loved for so long…

BOOKS   ZINES   NOVELS   COMICS

THE SATANIC SCREEN by Nikolas Schrek (2024 Headpress / 434 pages)

I missed out on the first edition from 2001, and here the author expands almost each chapter with relevant updates. Most notable (and informative) are the early sections dealing with literature and the silent film era and the massive number of occult themes used within them, and the section on 1990s/2000s evangelical films such as THE OMEGA CODE.

In the author's coverage of later films, he gave me a new appreciation of THE NINTH GATE, and delivers a fine, in-depth look at 2015's THE WITCH.

THE SATANIC SCREEN is a lengthy volume, filled with plenty of useful information you're not likely to come across on an Internet search. While I enjoyed Schrek's sarcasm, wit, and zeal (a complaint I've seen in several reviews of the first edition), I can see touchy readers being turned off by it. I didn't find it a problem, even when fun films like GHOST RIDER (2007) get trashed. (However, I'd bet the author would appreciate the occult-rich 70s comic series the film was based upon).

Fans of THE EXORCIST will likely disagree with the author's assessment of it, yet Schrek brings up several solid points to defend his edgy opinions. My main interest was the 60s and 70s era, and here the book shines, giving some of the best commentary available on ROSEMARY'S BABY as well as the barrage of exploitation films that were unleashed shortly thereafter.

An essential, well-written read, this is easily one of the finest works on occult cinema.

PURE: THE SEXUAL REVOLUTIONS OF MARILYN CHAMBERS BY Jared Stearns (2024 Headpress / 320 pages)

Intensely researched and an obvious labor or love, Stearns' biography of cinema's most famous adult film actress informs and entertains as it reveals a woman who managed to *almost* have it all.

From her groundbreaking porn films in the 70s, to her made-for-cable sex comedies and the couple attempts to break into the mainstream, PURE presents Chambers as a woman with not only a serious work ethic (be it on film or stage), but a loving friend and family member who went out of her way to help those around her in need. While she struggled through some abusive relationships, she always strived for professionalism, and battled demons when finally settling down to raise her daughter.

Packed with documented insights and notes from those close to her, PURE is the portrait of a pioneering performer who lived her life to the fullest while standing up for the rights of others. An all-around outstanding debut by Stearns.

THE SAVAGE SWORD OF CONAN (Titan Comics): Shortly after acquiring CONAN from Marvel Comics, Titan began a new chapter in our favorite Cimmerian's life in a regular comic book series, but Titan proceeded to bring back the magazine-sized SAVAGE SWORD OF CONAN in 2024, and the first 3 issues are well done. Anyone who remembers SAVAGE SWORD's original run knows you were in for a bit more than you'd get in the regular comic series, as the writing and artwork were often more brutal and in tune with Robert Howard's original stories. The first three issues feature fantastic writing by John Arcudi, Jim Zub, and Frank Tieri, and while the artwork is sometimes lacking, plenty is fantastic thanks to artists Max Von Fafner and Alan Quah. While I'm not a big fan of each issue's second feature, SOLOMON KANE, I must give credit to a fine job done by author/writer Patrick Zircher, who I wish they'd use to illustrate the main Conan tales. Either way, Titan has done a great job with both their Conan titles, but SAVAGE SWORD is a real treat for fans who may miss the glory days of old school magazines.

(Titan Books has also released three Conan novels so far, including S.M. Sterling's CONAN: BLOOD OF THE SERPENT, John C. Hocking's CONAN: CITY OF THE DEAD (which includes the author's praised 1995 novel 'Conan and the Emerald Lotus' along with its all-new sequel), and James Lovegrove's CONAN: CULT OF THE OBSIDIAN MOON. My main gripe here is the second two novels are deserving of much better covers, which has always been a staple of any Conan series, but so far the stories themselves have been solid.)

A WHOLE BAG OF CRAZY PART DEUX: ONE LAST TOKE: MORE STORIES OF WEED, HOOKERS, CONVENTIONS & GRINDHOUSE MOVIES by Pete Chiarella (2024 / 364 pages) is "42nd Street Pete" Chiarella's follow up to his 2018 memoir A WHOLE BAG OF CRAZY, this time featuring a lengthy section on his time working NJ and Ohio horror conventions, more vintage stories from the frontlines of 42nd Street back in its heyday, fans of the VHS days will love hearing more from Pete's days working at Liquidators, and some great wrestling stuff, which Pete was also heavily involved with. Slasher fans are in for a treat, as the author recollects countless screenings he attended in the late 70s/early 80s, and there's an informative section on Grindhouse westerns. The final few chapters are especially touching (and hilarious), as Pete brings some things to mind younger fans of this stuff need to consider. His capsule thoughts on the many film people he has met over the years are priceless (his opinion of Linda Blair cracked me up … but having met her I'm unfortunately in agreement). As an attendee of both the Son of Horrorthon and Chiller Theater conventions throughout the 90s and most of the early 2000s, Pete's account of what happened to him there pisses me off, but it's nice to at last hear the full story. I'm now twice as glad I stopped going to this once-great con.

A heavy tome filled with lots of rare pictures (including some 42nd Street marquees you most likely haven't seen before), this is a must read for those who like to hear what Times Square (and the seedier parts of NJ) were like before gentrification from someone who was *actually there*. Grab your copy at 42ndStreetPete.net.

INCIDENTS AROUND THE HOUSE by Josh Malerman (2024 Del Rey / 373 pages)

This haunted house/possession hybrid, told from the viewpoint of a young girl named Bela, may just possibly be the scariest horror novel so far this millennium … and I say this as a fan of horror fiction since 1976.

Bela lives in a two story home with her parents (Mommy and Daddo, as she refers to him), and has a secret friend who lives in her closet who she calls "Other Mommy." What begins as a friendly relationship eventually becomes sinister to the point her family goes on the run, but realize they need to face this thing head on in the hopes of ever having a normal life again.

Filled with great takes on every childhood fear and worry, Malerman delivers images that won't be leaving your psyche anytime soon, and one scene dealing with an amateur paranormal investigator delivers a wicked twist.

There are secrets, surprises, and scares at nearly every turn, and the overall creepiness factor here has just upped the genre big time.

This is the epitome of an instant classic.

SWEDISH CULTS by Anders Fager (2022 Valencourt Books / 230 pages) is a 2009 short story collection, considered a classic of Swedish horror, and in 2022 Valancourt Books translated it for English audiences.

'The Furies from Borås' features a group of club-hopping girls who worship a slime monster who lives in the woods. Picture the film 'The Craft' mixed with an extreme anime and that barely begins to describe this gruesome opener, full of sex, drugs, rock n roll ... and lots of tentacles. 'Fragment I', the first of four very short tales between the five longer stories, follows two senior cultists who can't seem to be able to retire.

'Grandma's Journey' finds two members of a pack (obviously werewolves, unless the author is using his animal descriptions metaphorically in dealing with immigrants), who travel from somewhere in Sweden to Yugoslavia to retrieve their grandmother from an isolated monastery. Along the way they pick up female slaves from Serbian gangsters and live on sausages and cola from gas stations. This one is quite strange and lengthy, yet impossible to put down. I'm still trying to figure out the (I think) cosmic ending. A minesweeping ship becomes the target of a gigantic sea creature in 'Fragment II,' and somehow Fager makes this 6-paged tale genuinely scary.

With the help of a legendary creature, a Norwegian man gets revenge on the Swedish army who slaughtered his family in 'The Broken Man's Wish.' Isolation, a shaman and a snowy landscape provide perfect reading for a cold New Year's Eve (in which the story is set around). 'Fragment III' listens in on two gang leaders discussing the psychos who robbed and mutilated one of their associates. This one's frustrating as it feels like a small piece of a bigger story, but judging from this five-page snippet the author could easily craft a full-length Swedish mob novel.

A semi-gold digger gets way more than she bargained for in 'Happy Forever On Östermalm,' arguably the best of the collection. Sex, horror, and vintage wine have never been so terrifying than in this gruesome take on queer horror. In 'Fragment IV,' a grandfather calls his seldom-seen granddaughter and pleads with her not to attend an event. Is he a terrorist? Hit man? This final brief fragment also feels like a novel excerpt, and I was thinking the author added these snippets for filler, until we discover this 4-page piece is a precursor to the final, lengthy entry, 'Miss Witt's Great Work,' in which a gallery owner/artist named My gains fame after a set of pornographic photos, featuring herself, is purchased by the leader of a strange cult. The cult influences her to create something truly different and risqué, and My gets to show it off during a televised evening talk show.

SWEDISH CULTS, despite some minor issues I'm sure are due to the translation, displays the work of a gifted writer who knows how to craft some serious chills. A couple of stories may feel a bit misogynist, but stick through to the end of them and you'll be treated to a fresh take on Lovecraftian horror you surely haven't experienced before. An all-around impressive collection.

DEAD MALL (written by Adam Cesare, art by David Stoll / 2023 Dark Horse Comics / 128 pages)

It's no easy feat to set a horror story in a mall without bringing to mind a couple of horror film classics, but Adam Cesare has managed to create something original here. This is a great coming of age tale that takes a couple of tropes and turns them on their heads.

With wonderful artwork by David Stoll, DEAD MALL is a solid graphic novel chiller filmmakers should jump on ASAP.

LET'S GO PLAY AT THE ADAMS' by Mendal W. Johnson (1974 Crowell, new edition 2023 Quirk Books / 277 pages)

This controversial novel, long out of print and found for big bucks on the secondhand market, was given new life thanks to Grady Hendrix' "Paperbacks from Hell" book and now retro book line.

Barbara, a 20-year-old babysitter, finds herself the hostage of 5 kids ranging in age from 10-17. They keep her bound and gagged while the parents of the Adams children are away for two weeks. It's all part of some twisted game the children have created, one that's never fully explained … and this will either irk the reader or draw them closer to the page.

Johnson keeps the tension and suspense relentless, leading to a finale that has divided many. I found it creepy, ahead of its time, and beyond evil. While the story gets a bit graphic at times, the power here is in the psychological downfall of Barbara, and the children who have convinced themselves this babysitter is little more than a device to be used for their own amusement and discovery.

Originally released 15 years before Jack Ketchum's infamous THE GIRL NEXT DOOR, this is quite similar, and some reviews claim they're both based on the same true life story. This may feel dated to some, but it's still a precursor to what would become known as "extreme horror," and it has held up well as a genuinely disturbing read.

Quirk Books' 2023 edition features an informative introduction, and it was sad to learn the author died shortly after the book was published. I can only imagine what else was hiding in his twisted mind.

OUR FIRST ISSUE is available on Amazon and at better book and comic stores.

COMING SOON: ISSUE THREE features an article on George A. Romero's MARTIN and the weird vampire films of the 70s, plus the 82nd edition of SUBURBAN GRINDHOUSE MEMORIES looks at the insane JUNGLE WARRIORS…

Printed in Great Britain
by Amazon